Existential Systemic Therapy

Jason Dias

University of the Rockies

Submitted in partial fulfillment of the requirements for a

Doctorate in Clinical Psychology

June, 2010

Approved: Date:

_____   _____

_____   _____

_____   _____

Acknowledgements and Dedications

I would like to thank firstly my Dissertation Committee. Dick Gee, chairperson, has been enormously (and perhaps unconsciously) influential along the way. His ideas of working playfully, of being spontaneous, and his ability to make me see myself as others see me – thus calling me to account for my own freedom/responsibility – these things have been foundational in my education. I can only hope they have also found their way into this work in some measure.

Louis Hoffman has also been very influential. If there is such a thing as Karma, I have incurred quite a debt for the good fortune Dr. Hoffman has made possible. His insistence that students have the opportunity to attend conferences and to share in his love affair with China have really kept me both excited and focused. In addition, his role as a mentor has been very important. Dr. Hoffman has supported me gently every step of the way, respectful of my feelings, my opinions, my presence. He has embodied Existentialism in an awe-filled, presenceful manner at every turn.

Justin Lincoln has also, in his way, guided my practice. His honest critiques and his way of being present to his students again embodies what he is about and provides some of the basis for the exploration of authenticity contained herein. His belief that qualitative measures have a significant place in research and his respect for each student's way of encountering their self in their work is a profound influence. In class he took the somewhat extraordinary measure of bringing each student an article selected to coincide with the student's peculiar interests; I was suitably impressed with this thoughtfulness (and have included the article he recommended in this text).

Next, I would like to thank the people I have worked with closely in the last year or so. Michael Moats has become like something of a brother through close association. I have bounced a multitude of ideas off of him and he has always patiently and respectfully responded, sometimes positively and sometimes with constructive critique. These writings are substantively a summary of our conversations over the last four years.

Trent Claypool has been influential in the same manner. We have been in the same classes, the same practicum, the same international conferences for several years. It has been my pleasure to grow by observing his own dedicated self-development, and to talk about these ideas along the way.

Dave Elkins was another profound, if all-too-brief influence. His fiery brand of radical humanism, his passion for being not just helpful to people but good to them, is an inspiration. In the end he set a fitting example.

I would like to thank Tom Greening for sharing of himself during our encounters and Karen Kissel-Wigela for some rather frank and intense discussions during a Division 32 conference.

I would also like to mention the people at Franciscan Community Counseling, where I have been an intern during the writing of this dissertation. The people I have worked with have been open-minded, helpful and quite welcoming. I would specifically like to acknowledge the aid of Judith Schaeffer. Co-therapy and supervision with Dr. Schaeffer have been eye-opening and confidence building. Moreover, she has aided to the shaking up of my preconceptions several times over the past year, for which I will be ever grateful.

In China, I had the privilege to meet and converse with many fine colleagues for the purposes of dialogue and mutual brain-picking. Zhengjia Ren remains a close friend and solid influence: many dissertations committee will be reading the words, "Psychology is dogshit" this season. Aside from being a Chinese national hero, he is also a great soul. Mark Yang has spent the past two years seducing me on behalf of China, for which I will always be grateful. And Wang Xeufu, while often quiet and mysterious, embodies Chinese existentialism like no other person.

Finally, I would like to thank Kirk Schneider for his interest in my generation of students entering the field. His devotion to spreading the word about Existentialism is laudable, and the relationship he has developed with University of the Rockies has been fruitful. Moreover, his willingness to take a personal interest in me and my work despite his own intense workload has helped me resolve to get this thing done.

This dissertation is dedicated to my wife and son, without whom I would be perfectly content flipping burgers.

For copies of this work, please contact Jason Dias at JasonE.Dias@gmail.com.

Abstract

This dissertation explores the integration of Existential methods and Family Systems therapy by reviewing the existing literature on each methodology. It then examines parallels and underlying themes. It finds substantial confluence between the philosophy and methods of the authors reviewed, notes these points of commonality as well as points of disparity, and begins to form the basis for a theory of Existential Systemic Therapy (ExiST). Fundamentally, it reduces a large amount of theoretical data into a series of stances that the ExiST practitioner might adopt with respect to work with families.

Existential Systemic Therapy (ExiST)

Prologue: Consider the Trees

Imagine a tree whose trunk is Existential Psychotherapy. The trunk appears solid and distinct, an individual entity. But follow the trunk higher until it begins to separate into principles like presence and authenticity – in other words, branches. Sometimes the branches cross with the branches of other trees. These entanglements we see are times when two competing theories are talking about the same idea in different terms. For example, Existential theory is entangled with Systemic theory when one discusses authenticity and the other talks about congruence: one idea with two names.

Imagine now backing away from the trees but keeping them in view. One begins to observe not just two trees but many, a whole grove of them. Where their branches are entangled visibly, their roots are entangled invisibly. Indeed, if one could dig beneath the trees and examine the roots closely, one would find that the roots are not merely entangled but shared in common.

The aspen tree gives the appearance of being a distinct entity. However, when we examine the roots we find that the aspen grove is all one huge living being, no tree separate from any other tree in the grove.

In this way too, we can discover that themes in Existentialism and in Systemic work are not just similar or held in common but based on more basic roots, more basic theories. As we uncover these roots perhaps we will find out what it is that makes psychotherapy work–not only Existential or Systemic therapy but all psychotherapy.

Background of Problem

Science is a system of thought based on a collection of values; these values are as baseless as any other set of values and yet have proven fruitful in examining and understanding the world and making predictions about future events. This is to say science based on these values has predictive value and pragmatic value. Quantum Physics, for example, gives us color television; while mind-bending and paradoxical, it is useful. One of the core values of scientific inquiry is that a theory should explain as much as possible in the simplest terms. Thus the first international science celebrity, Albert Einstein, is famous for his equation $E=mc^2$ (Brallier & Parker, 2002, p. 47). While few people know what it means, most everyone has heard of it. These five characters explain a fundamental principle of the universe and have application almost everywhere.

While there is a certain danger in referring to physics as the nadir model of science, these references are offered as a metaphor. Physics, too, has given us failures: the atomic bomb, while technically wondrous, is less than wonderful; Einstein's theory of relativity has application only on large scales; string field theory, which initially offered hope of providing the "theory of everything," a one-inch-long equation that will account for all the phenomena we can observe, actually has produced tens of thousands of equations that rely on reified phenomena such as alternate universes.

Thus, while this paper is inspired by the need to cleave more closely to the values and philosophy of science, it does not aspire to be physics. Moreover, of fecundity, disprovability, reproducibility, utility and elegance, this paper will attempt mostly to live up to the values of utility and, especially, elegance.

The field of psychology is progressing along a path opposite this core value while at the same time espousing it. The goal of a clinician using the *Diagnostic and Statistical Manual*, for example, is differential diagnosis: the process of explaining as much of the patient's condition as possible using the fewest labels (American Psychiatric Association [*DSM-IV-TR*], 2000). The field of psychotherapy is becoming cluttered with competing approaches, each seeming to vie for theoretical supremacy, profitability, and increasing specificity. Schneider (2008) suggests, "We will soon be, if we are not already, threatened by a chaos of competing practices" (p. 15). Elkins (2009) suggests that all these competing points of view are generally of equal worth. Drawing on theoretical and empirical literature, he goes on to distill the research and discuss the "contextual factors" that really lead to change. In addition, he proposes a sort of radical humanism to offset the forces that have worked to medicalize the psychology industry. In this dissertation, however, it is proposed that the only cure for disintegration is reintegration. That is, as humanistic and medical psychology vie for dominance, making treatment a political issue is damaging to both fields. As Schneider (2008) suggests, Existential thought is the most influential and yet least publicly embraced of the schools of therapy; thus we might use this pervasive influence and presence not to unseat medically oriented practice but to understand it more clearly and, in turn, be more understood. Or, to quote Elkins (2009), he would encourage those drawn to medical model, short-term treatments,

> ...to consider embedding these in a broader, more complex theoretical framework such as that which Humanistic-Existential [HE] psychology provides. Historically, HE psychology welcomed diverse therapeutic approaches and there is no reason that it cannot integrate CBT and other short-term approaches into its

framework…. This does not mean that HE should "swallow whole" any therapeutic approach that comes along, but it does mean that we should always be open to a careful, thoughtful integration of any perspective that does not, within itself, undermine humanistic principles and that can make useful contributions to the therapeutic endeavor. (p. 38)

Moreover, in reviewing the work of Wampold (2001), Elkins concludes:

The results were clear and unambiguous: the scientific evidence showed that the contextual model is correct and the medical model is wrong. In other words, the evidence showed that it is not techniques that are responsible for therapeutic outcome but certain other factors in the therapeutic situation that are common to all therapeutic systems. (Italics in original, p. 70)

Thus the real value of psychotherapy is some underlying principle or set of principles. What is the $E=mc^2$ of psychotherapy?

This project, then, attempts to broaden the scope of Existential practice into the treatment of families by discovering Existential themes in that venue. While this dissertation focuses on family treatment, it is hoped that others with more expertise in the more medicalized fields will take this project as an example and proceed with coherent integration. An excellent start has been made in Schneider's (2008) *Existential Integrative Psychotherapy: Guideposts to the Core of Practice*. In this volume, many authors contribute rational integrations of Existential thought into other realms of practice; this dissertation will hopefully contribute another dimension to that work.

If there are common roots (and routes) to psychopathology and dysfunction, then scientific method suggests common factors should be present when disparate treatments result in alleviation of the problem. Indeed, the corpus of work by Carl Rogers suggests exactly this: that factors local to the client or patient and the therapist account for more success in therapy than specific method. A more recent meta-analysis (Wampold, 2001) demonstrates again that the so-called "contextual factors" are more important than the exact methodology in use.

For the Existential practitioner, and this is the core of the problem and reason for writing this dissertation, there exists no lucid guide to family practice in an Existential context that integrates the volumes of theory on both sides of the equation. Thus a specialist in Existential treatment has no or limited rational basis for the treatment of families or family problems without further specializations. If one major contextual factor is one's expertise and belief in one's treatment modality, then surely providing treatment with no theoretical base is treating out of context.

Recent meta-analysis found that belief in one's treatment modality accounts for more outcome variance than treatment modality itself (Norcross, 2008). If one accepts the view that multiple specializations dilute the theory and that dilution of theory results in weaker practice, then having a specific Existential method for Systemic work might result in better outcomes for Existential practitioners.

A possible explanation for the importance of theory to context is easily found. For example, Yalom (1980) suggests that having a solid theoretical grounding is of use to the clinician in being of service to the client, regardless of the empirical truth of the system. He states that coherent interpretations on the part of the clinician will tend to empower the client, providing insight that catalyzes change. No one system of thought

(Psychoanalytic vs. Jungian, for example) has the rights to *the truth*; rather the interpretation need only have explanatory power to be of benefit to the client.

Similarly, the clinician needs a framework of interpretation in order to be empowered to help the client. Yalom (1980) says:

> The importance of such an explanatory system is as important for the therapist as it is for the patient. Every therapist uses an explanatory system – some ideological frame of reference – to organize the clinical material with which they are faced. Even if the therapist's explanatory system is so complex and abstract and so rooted in unconscious structures that it cannot be explicitly transmitted to the patient, it nonetheless enhances the therapist's effectiveness in numerous ways. (p. 190)

These numerous ways include the ability to compartmentalize the patient's "clinical material" in such a way that is it not overwhelming to the practitioner; this in turn allows the therapist to create a safe space and foster a strong relationship; it further allows the therapist to demonstrate understanding of and normalize the patient's problems; it increases the placebo effect (i.e., the therapist is confident in their abilities and this confidence reaches the patient); it gives the therapist and the patient something to do while the real change agent works (that is, focusing on the material suggested by the clinical theory gives us a shared project around which to grow an alliance); it permits consistency on the part of the therapist (Yalom, 1980).

Elkins (2009) also comments on the need for a rational set of procedures:

> On the other hand, while they have no inherent power to heal, theories and techniques do contribute to therapeutic outcome by providing a credible rationale

and set of procedures that serve as a vehicle for the therapeutic work and by expressing, and serving as a conduit for, other factors in the therapeutic situation known to be responsible for outcome. In other words, in their role and function as contextual factors found in all therapeutic systems, theories and techniques *do* contribute to therapeutic outcome. (p. 74)

Therefore the necessity of a theoretical grounding in therapy is difficult to overstate; given that this thesis will likely fall very short of the mark of comprehensiveness, it is hoped that it will provoke further inquiry into the Existential practice of Family Systems work.

Purpose and Importance of Study

This dissertation will elucidate and integrate Existential theory and methodology with Family Systems theory and practice. With the discovery of the underlying factors that make various types of treatment successful, treatments can be tailored to those factors. This examination should prove profitable in terms of shining a light on the similarities and differences between two treatment modalities that seem disparate at first glance. Moreover, a rational method of Family Systems practice seems needed for the Existential provider.

Finally, and at the radical humanism level perhaps suggested by Elkins (2009), a long-range purpose is to begin the process of drawing together all the parts of psychotherapy that have proliferated and cast themselves away in the call of specificity. As in a pre dark-matter view of the universe, all the stars and constellations and galaxies have spun away as far as they can, and it is time for them to come back together in a "big crunch." As each theoretical system merges with others, it must shed its specific techniques and yield back to the whole the general principles it has learned; as these are found to be in common, it will reinforce the common themes; as these are found to be disparate, the examination of the differences will be of great profit. And, in the end, when there are no specific schools of thought left, we will be left with $E=mc^2$.

Research Questions

The major topics of research at hand are: how are Existential philosophy and Family Systems philosophy similar, and how do they differ? And, how are Existential Psychotherapy theory and Family Systems theory similar, and how do they differ?

Clarification of Terms

Existential. Concerned with the ultimate givens of existence; the field of psychotherapy concerned with the philosophical aspects of being, such as the meaning of life and death, the paradox of being meaning-seeking beings in a banal universe, and the nature of free will and agency.

Existentialism. The philosophical study of Existential concerns.

Existential Psychotherapy. The application of Existentialism in a therapeutic context to problems of living.

Family Systems Therapy. The field of psychotherapy concerned with the interactions of family members and their treatment as a group, unit or gestalt.

Systemic Thought. The philosophic inquiry into how families form and maintain systems.

Integrative. Putting together two or more systems of thought into a coherent whole with more explanatory power and utility than either system alone.

Synthesis. A third idea generated as a result of trying to merge two ideas.

Summary

There is a need for an integrated theory of Existential and Systemic thought and practice in order that Existential Psychotherapy purveyors have a rational basis of practice when working with families. Moreover, there is a need to counteract a wider trend in psychotherapy at large away from integration, towards disintegration.

This dissertation examines points of commonality and points of divergence between Existentialism and Systemic thought as well as between the theories of Existential Psychotherapy and Family Systems Therapy.

Chapter II selectively reviews literature from Existential and Systemic sources, as well as idiographic sources that bear on the problem. Chapter III outlines the methods used to distill general principles from that data. Chapter IV uses those methods to that end. Chapter V produces a synthesis from those general principles, a unique third theory that is hopefully more basic, more fundamental than either previous theory. It also describes the personal lessons the author learned while doing this project, and points to future research questions this project might provoke.

Literature Review

This chapter examines the pertinent literature about Existentialism, Existential Psychotherapy, Systemic thought and Family Systems therapy from Irvin Yalom, Kirk Schneider, Victor Frankl, Rollo May, Murray Bowen, Virginia Satir, Carl Whitaker, Salvadore Minuchin, Ronald "R. D." Laing and Frederick "Fritz" Perls. It will highlight the major contributions from each theorist. In addition, each new idea is tagged to identify confluence with other ideas from other authors.

It is hoped that this chapter will clarify and distill many of the ideas involved in the two systems of philosophy and theory down to a number of useable, easily understood concepts. Later, these concepts will be used to suggest a third paradigm that weaves together the most useful of the ideas from each discipline.

Irvin Yalom

Yalom's version of Existentialism is remarkably pervasive and yet misunderstood. It is easy to be exposed to many of his interpersonal ideas as Existential ones. This confusion probably stems from a lack of clarity on Yalom's part, as cited in a footnote to *The Gift of Therapy* (Yalom, 2003/2009; p. 4 of post script). He says here that he has never considered Existentialism to be a freestanding school of thought and that the ideas he has put forward in so many books are intended to be useful in all forms of therapy.

This leaves the author with a bit of a dilemma: accept that only parts of his writing pertain to Existentialism and that others are more germane to Interpersonal theory or Psychodynamic thought; alternatively, take the position that Yalom has been so influential on Existential thought that his ideas from other venues have been integrated as a whole into Existentialism. As this project is aimed at a larger target than the two schools under survey here, some contamination from Interpersonal or Psychodynamic thought only serves the greater purpose.

Everyone faces the same ultimate concerns. The ultimate concerns, usually referred to as the Existential Givens, appear early in Yalom's work and are largely the content of his *Existential Psychotherapy* (Yalom, 1980). They are: Isolation, Freedom/Responsibility, Meaninglessness, and Death.

Yalom (1980) suggests these themes arise over and over again through the course of any type of psychotherapy, and that it behooves therapists to become attuned to these issues. He takes the Psychodynamic position that sometimes issues stand in for other issues. For example, a client who comes to us for help with generalized anxiety might be experiencing a pervasive dread. While Freud might explain that dread with castration anxiety, Yalom suggests the subject of the dread is really death, and cites numerous cases (p 58-74) of Freud omitting references to death from his patients.

For Yalom, Death is the ultimate Ultimate Concern; all concerns can be boiled down, essentially, to death anxiety. But he does not downplay the importance of the other concerns.

For Yalom, the process of psychopathology is somewhat akin to, but not entirely like, the system of repressions and defenses and drives set up by Freud. How death factors into a person's life, for example, is a matter of how it is experienced (or not) in early childhood. How parents teach a child about death and dying, both explicitly and implicitly, as well as the child's own experiences with bereavement will impact how the adult later copes with the inevitability of annihilation.

Similarly, the way the child encounters their own independence and agency and the way the parent figures help the child slowly fledge will later impact the adult's conflicts with freedom and responsibility; likewise the conflict between the need for connectedness and the fact of isolation.

Yalom (1980) posits two main defenses against these ultimate concerns: merging and the hero fantasy. By merging with another person, one can subsume one's own ego functions–giving them responsibility for one's own choices, connectedness, meaning and continuation and effectively blinding oneself to the limitations one faces. By believing one will ultimately be rescued by a powerful figure, one can similarly ignore the inevitable conclusion to life.

He suggests these defenses are largely dysfunctional and that the cure is authentic engagement with these insoluble limitations.

Yalom (1980) is clear on the idea that there may be other existential givens. One example, according to Hoffman (2009), is embodiment. Drawing on a number of sources, such as the work of Bugental and Heery as well as Nietzsche and Kierkegaard, Hoffman suggests that embodiment or emotions are the manner in which one lives in awareness of death or limitation, meaninglessness, isolation and responsibility. That is to say, how these givens are embodied. He suggests they are lived primarily through emotions; thus we need to begin to become aware of and make friends with our emotions. Anxiety is archetypal in this endeavor, and will be discussed in greater detail when we come to Rollo May later in this discussion.

Related ideas can be found in Schneider (liberation, vivifying and confronting resistances and self-protections, paradox, meaning, constriction vs. expansion); Frankl (meaning, freedom); May (courage, angst, anxiety, will); Satir (freedom and responsibility); Whitaker (family life cycle, givens of family existence, myth); Minuchin (family life cycle, family myth and narrative).

All problems are interpersonal problems. Yalom treats all problems from an interpersonal perspective. Depression, he suggests, can be viewed as a problem of interaction; for example, "passive dependency, isolation, obsequiousness, inability to express anger, hypersensitivity to separation…" (Yalom, 2005, p 24). Diagnostic labels become somewhat unimportant and sometimes even counterproductive (Yalom, 2003, p. 4). The therapy is about a gradual unfolding of the relationship and an opportunity to examine and intervene with interpersonal problems in the here and now (1980, p. 182).

Rather than focusing on pathology and cure, Yalom suggests the concerns noted above (or at least that the way the person engages or refuses to engage with the concerns) are the problem, and that the problem perpetuates and is perpetuated by the way the person engages with others. For example, a person terrified of death might seek to have only short relationships, in order to never lose a loved one to death and thus escape the reminder of their own mortality. This person will engage others in a way specifically intended to keep them at arm's length, to prevent attachment.

These ideas are especially germane to group psychotherapy and, by association, to family therapy. According to Yalom (2005, p. 97) the group therapy process is overshadowed by the ghosts of families past, and the context of group therapy is one in which Family Systems are replayed out of context and corrected. The "corrective recapitulation of the family experience," while not rated as very powerful by therapy-goers, is rated by Yalom as intrinsic to the process (2005, p. 97). He does not comment on the possibility of corrective family process in context, that is, in the presence of the family process.

Moreover, the group process puts the therapy-goers in direct contact with the ultimate concerns (2005). The group process itself intrinsically brings this contact about. As the group begins to work together they go through stages; they inquire more and more about one another's problems and learn to trust and share those problems. They learn through this sharing that some limited contact with others is possible-and they learn how they fear that contact and make it impossible. As the group members try to solve one another's problems through advice-giving, they learn how they are essentially isolated, that one cannot live life for or merge with another person. As group members drop out, the group learns how to cope with the temporariness of all relationships and even with death. Freedom and responsibility are naturally included in the process as interpersonal choices are rewarded with interpersonal consequences and opportunities for engagement can be taken or refused or modified. Meanings are assigned and negotiated. When the Ultimate Concerns become the focus of the process, Yalom calls this "boundary territory," and it presents the opportunity to work directly with the givens of existence.

These things all happen in the 1:1 therapy relationship also. However, with only one target for transference or conflict or engagement, the opportunities to learn these sorts of lessons come along less frequently.

Related ideas can be found in May (encounter); Bowen (differentiation and nuclear family emotional system); Satir (connectedness and experiential learning); Whitaker (use of self in therapy and doing one's own work, symbolic experiential therapy, directiveness); Minuchin (joining the system, family pathology, experiential approach); Laing (mental illness) and Perls (encounter).

Authenticity. Yalom rarely addresses the issue of authenticity directly. Rather, he writes about the factors that lead to the authentic engagement and the power of that engagement, both in fiction and non-fiction. The issue of authenticity is entangled with that of the therapy relationship inasmuch as authenticity is meaningless without engagement, and engagement must take place in a relational context. *Lying on the Couch* (Yalom, 1996), for example, is primarily about a female therapy-goer (Carol) who attends therapy out of spite for the therapist. Her attendance is not aimed at curing herself of her obvious pathology but at tricking the therapist into mistakes she can use against him in a lawsuit. The therapist, Dr. Ernest Lash, has at the same moment decided to be completely honest and forthright with the next patient to enter his office. Thus Yalom describes the power of interpersonal honesty in the healing relationship as Carol is slowly changed by Lash's honest and often provocative engagements. Yalom (2003) says of this work:

> One of my major intentions in this novel is to affirm that therapist authenticity will ultimately be redemptive even under the worst circumstances – that is, a clinical encounter with a scheming pseudo-patient. (p. 82)

In *When Nietzsche Wept* (Yalom, 2005), the plot is somewhat reversed; the psychotherapist attempts to heal the cantankerous patient (in this case, Friedrich Nietzsche) without Nietzsche's consent or knowledge. In attempting to explain a possible origin of psychotherapy, Yalom again puts forth the power of the honest relationship to heal. As Nietzsche engages with the doctor, he learns about himself and his own needs; the doctor is similarly enlightened by his encounters with Nietzsche. The ultimate test of the healing power of honesty comes at the end of the novel when the doctor reveals to the Professor the ruse, the false relationship that was set up to provide the window of opportunity for the real relationship.

This theme of candor and honesty is present throughout Yalom's work, along with the idea that the necessary candor requires quite a bit of interpersonal courage. He suggests that this courage is not always accessible at the right time, that it requires a sort of heroism on the part of the therapist to perpetrate and on the part of the client to utilize.

He lists many of the components of his own personal brand of authenticity in *The Gift of Therapy* (Yalom, 2002). He begins with the idea of the therapist and patient as fellow travelers; the therapist is not in a superordinate position but rather accompanies the patient for a short time as they examine their problem. The therapist knows that there but for the grace of god go I. Thus, authentic engagement does not include power games or hierarchy.

The next component is engagement. Yalom (1980) suggests that many patients have difficulty engaging in intimate relationships and that the remedy for this difficulty is simply to engage in an intimate relationship with the therapist. The therapist must engage the patient at the deepest possible level (within the boundaries and context of the therapeutic relationship) and do this always kindly and with the best interest of the patient at heart.

This in part means being supportive and empathetic. One need not support the person's behavior to support the person, but one must always support the person. Often, making the attempt to enter their personal world, to see from their point of view and know their feelings, is support enough. And the act of empathy teaches the power of empathy in relatedness.

The next component is letting the patient matter to you. Remaining unworldly, distant and disengaged is not likely to be a good recipe for empathy and support. The patient needs to feel cared about and that care needs to be authentic; thus the person must have the power to affect the therapist in some fashion. This facilitates interpersonal learning (1980).

While Carl Whitaker would suggest that this interpersonal learning is implicit and non-verbal, Yalom advocates the position of making things more conscious. Thus while Whitaker would simply react to his patients, Yalom articulates how the person has affected him. Part of being authentic is honesty about one's reactions to other people; thus the hurtful act is met with a comment as much as is the charitable act.

Included in this honesty is humility; that is, one is accountable for one's mistakes. Part of the process of therapy and the relationship is making mistakes and talking about them. Humility is learned through humility, but also the therapeutic relationship is likely to be deeper when the patient knows he or she can fully trust the therapist. This lack of attachment to rightness, this vulnerability to the patient, encourages a like vulnerability in return.

One must also act according to one's stated beliefs. Yalom suggests that the act must match the word; if one says one trusts the patient, this must be backed up with incidences of trustful behavior. While this idea is treated rather briefly, it is the core of what Virginia Satir called "Congruence," (Baldwin, 1999) and will surface again later in this document as a key idea in Systemic thinking.

Yalom also suggests that the idea of the therapist as tabula rasa – the blank slate or blank screen-is outdated and unhelpful. Part of authenticity is acknowledging one's own thoughts, feelings, reactions. This idea may not be very separate from engagement; being with requires being, fundamentally, and the tabula rasa is a way of denying being. Thus disclosure begets disclosure; one helps the patient to open up by opening up.

Related ideas can be found in Schneider (invoking the actual, vivifying and confront resistances and self-protections); May (courage, The Daimonic); Bowen (triangles); Satir (congruence, the monad); Whitaker (use of self in therapy and doing one's own work, personal involvement); Minuchin (read this book and forget about it); Laing (mental illness).

The healing relationship. Yalom is convinced that the relationship between the therapist and the patient is what heals. He notes:

> There is no more self-evident truth in psychotherapy; every therapist observes over and over in clinical work that the encounter itself is healing for the patient in a way that transcends the therapist's theoretical orientation.
>
> If any single fact has been established by psychotherapy research, it is that a positive relationship between patient and therapist is positively related to therapy outcome. Effective therapists respond to their patients in a genuine manner; they establish a relationship that a patient perceives as safe and accepting; they display a high degree of accurate empathy and are able to "be with" or "grasp the meaning" of a patient. (Yalom, 1980, p. 401)

Note the entanglement in Yalom's thinking between genuineness (authenticity) and the relationship. When discussing Yalom, it is difficult to mention one without the other.

Yalom (1980, p.404) goes on to suggest the mechanisms by which he thinks the relationship heals: by illuminating and facilitating other relationships, and through the communication inherent in the relationship itself. That is, in the first case, the patient relates to the therapist as if they are someone else in their life. The therapist helps the patient sort out how their behavior in this context is bringing about the problems the patient brought to therapy. In the second case, the ultimate concerns, the inescapable limitations of being, are faced by the therapist and patient side-by-side. Moreover, in either case, the patient and therapist move ever closer to Buber's ideal "I-Thou" relationship.

Yalom (1980) even goes so far as to suggest that all of the techniques of therapy-the analysis of dreams, the interpretations of patient action and verbal content, the data-gathering and rapport building–are all of value only inasmuch as they provide time and context for the healing relationship to develop and work. Like men playing checkers in the park, the game itself may be of limited importance; it is merely the context for a relationship.

He does suggest individual values for each of the activities of therapy, pointing out a paradox that appears in contextual factor research. As Elkins (2009) notes, the research indicates that specific techniques in themselves have no bearing on therapy effectiveness. However, therapist mastery of their chosen techniques does have some bearing on outcome. Thus, it matters very little what we do in therapy, and it matters somewhat more whether we are good at our chosen interventions.

Related ideas can be found in Schneider (awe); Frankl (meaning); May (encounter); Bowen (coaching, societal emotional process); Satir (connectedness and experiential learning); Whitaker (limited encounter, symbolic experiential treatment); Minuchin (joining the system, experiential approach); Perls (look inside, look outside, now I am aware…).

Interpretation. Yalom (1980, 2003) suggests that the role of interpretation is to (a) give the therapist a framework to understand the information they are taking on from the patient and (b) to give the patient the means to understand their own problem and behavior in a way that promotes self understanding and also a feeling of mastery. He makes it plain that he believes interpretation is important to the process of therapy and, as noted above, that it is ultimately done in the service of promoting a helpful relationship.

He also notes that The Truth is not the goal of interpretation (2003, p. 174). The truth as we see it may be less important than the patient's subjective experience, and our goal is always the best interest of the person-to which an objective truth must always come second. He notes that sometimes an intellectual search for truth can lead us away from the truth of the moment and occlude opportunities for relatedness.

Related ideas can be found in Schneider (the truth); May (myth); Whitaker (myths); Minuchin (diagrams, family myth and narrative).

The loan of life. Borrowing from various sources (perhaps especially Frankl, p. 137) Yalom suggests a third defense against the inevitable ultimate concerns: to avoid repaying the debt of death by refusing the gift of life. Enforcing self-isolation, for example, frees one from the future pain of loss (or the death of relationship). Refusal to risk frees one from the pain of failure (or the death of dreams, hope, and self-efficacy).

He uses several analogies to illuminate the preciousness of this gift of life and the desperateness of our choice regarding what to do with it. Referring to Nietzsche, for example, he suggests we consider the eternity of time that passed before we came into consciousness and the eternity that will happen after we have passed out of it. What, he wonders, is the significance of that tiny spark amid so much darkness? He suggests also that we consider another of Nietzsche's proposals: that a powerful being informs us that our lives would be repeated, unchanging in the slightest detail, over and over for eternity. Would we bless or curse this entity? And what choices would we make differently, knowing that we have to relive each moment over and over again?

Responsibility assumption. Yalom posits that every therapy contains some form of responsibility assumption as part of its cure. CBT, for example, makes patients responsible for their thought content; by actively changing the content, they can change the way they feel and act. DBT, meanwhile, makes people responsible for how they judge themselves and for how they interact with others.

For Yalom, there are at least two levels of responsibility. The first is fairly immediate: how one's actions impact the life one leads. This is easily elucidated through the therapy process, particularly with the models offered in group therapy. The assumption of responsibility for one's aloneness and meaninglessness are fairly straightforward in this context.

The second level is an Existential responsibility. Given the briefness of our time on Earth and the colossal coincidences that had to happen to bring about our being at just this time and in just this manner, are we not responsible to do with our lives something of importance? Can we in good conscience deny our freedom, give it away to other parties in order to deny responsibility for our choices? Can we in good conscience simply idle away our time, unhurried by the specter of death that hovers over every life?

This level of responsibility assumption is a bit more esoteric and is not often accessible through talk or techniques. Thus Yalom (1980) criticizes Frankl's Logotherapy as a blunt, authoritarian tool which offers the patient a meaning while stripping the patient further of their responsibility to discover this for themselves. (p.476) He suggests that the ability to create meaning in the face of certain annihilation is the product of a life lived well rather than simple exhortation, and that the process of therapy is a microcosm of life in which the patient has the opportunity to live well: by engaging more and more authentically with the therapist.

Yalom suggests that the inescapable problems of life are not the problem. We all face them and usually without pathology. Rather, the way the person engages with their problems is the problem. Thus, offering a simple solution to the problems (or exhorting to meaning) does away with the stimulus, but the response remains waiting in the wings.

Related ideas can be found in Schneider (liberation, vivifying and confronting resistances and self-protections); Frankl (freedom); May (angst, intentionality); Satir (Freedom and Responsibility) Whitaker (co-therapy); Minuchin (diagrams).

Here and now orientation and limited disclosure. Yalom posits that the most productive arena for interpersonal work is in the here and now. Questions of past experience, while important, can best be resolved in the present. This orientation is rooted in the belief that all problems are interpersonal problems (see above). The more the therapist can help the patient be authentic in this moment, the more the patient can choose how their past will influence the present.

Coupled with this idea is the technique of here and now disclosure. One invites the patient to speak of things as though they were happening now, or invites comment on the current process. Part of this invitation is commenting on one's own inner process as it happens. One's impressions or feelings regarding the patient become grist for the mill. This helps the patient decide whether the way they interact with others is effective.

Yalom recommends striking when the iron is cold (e.g. 2003/2009, p. 121). That is, one might comment on process when the patient has either run out of material or is filling the hour with irrelevant utterances. Process comments can tend to refocus the therapy on the here and now.

Part of the therapy process is the revelation of secrets, particularly from a group psychotherapy perspective (Yalom, 2005). Particularly germane to this revelation is the idea of horizontal disclosure. When a revelation is made, Yalom (and through Yalom, the group) seek more information not about the details of the item disclosed but about the disclosure itself. Questions, then, would focus not on vertical material: what happened, why it happened, how one felt about it happening, who was responsible, what is to be done about it. Rather, inquiry would be made about the disclosure itself: what allowed the person to finally reveal the secret in this company; how the person feels about revealing it; how the person feels about others in the room following their responses. The vertical material is considered voyeuristic; the latter material is considered means of deepening relationships and examining their limitations.

Related ideas can be found in Schneider (awe, invoking the actual, vivifying and confronting liberations and self-protections); May (centrality of being); Bowen (triangles, emotional cutoff); Whitaker (symbolic experiential treatment, limited encounter); Minuchin (diagrams, experiential approach); Perls (look inside, look outside, now I am aware).

Kirk Schneider

Integration. Schneider (2008; Schneider & Krug, 2010) espouses an Existential-Humanistic approach as a set of core skills or principles for any comparatively established therapeutic modality. Rather than thinking of Existential Psychotherapy as a stand-alone practice, he advocates a style of Existentialism he calls Existential-Integrative (EI) Psychotherapy, the core principles of which can be easily integrated into other models of practice.

The Primacy of Awe. Schneider (2008) lists four therapeutic factors as key to the experiential liberation that is core to the EI practice: presence, invoking the actual, vivifying and confronting resistance (or "self-protections"), and the rediscovery of meaning and awe. While awe is mentioned last, it is integral to the understanding of each of the other components. To be present, for example, requires that one abandon preconceptions to the extent possible. As knowledge precludes learning, so does foreknowledge of the other prevent encounter. To invoke the actual, one must first be open to the actual, and reverent of the actual. To dismiss a feeling or a thought as trivia or irrationality would upset the process. To vivify and confront resistance, one must first be able to engage with the resistance. This means one must also be able to abandon the need for control of the other.

Awe is so integral to the process that it is described first, to provide a context for the rest of Schneider's work.

Awe. Schneider (2004, 2010) suggests one attitude central to psychotherapeutic cure is "awe." For him, this word has layered meanings and connotations. In one sense, it conveys the ultimate dread and terror of being which must be engaged: the feeling one gets at seeing a tidal wave or tornado bearing down on them; the knowledge of our relative insignificance in the face of eternity and infinity; the knowledge of our ultimate powerlessness, perhaps sometimes in the face of god.

He suggests we consider not only that we are faced with this moment, sitting together engaged in conversation, but also that as we converse we are sitting in a room, in a building, in a city with hundreds of thousands of inhabitants going about their business; on a continent that is drifting slowly across the planet; that the planet is turning and whirling through an orbit; that the solar system is being carried through space at incalculable speed around a galactic central core which is itself in motion away from a universal center.

As we consider how small we are when scaled next to such grand objects as the galaxy and movements that begin with infinite smallness and end with dissolution, we might begin to feel the tickle of dread that is, in one sense, awe.

This awe is only one sense, one connotation, of the word. In another sense, he is describing the idea of being without asking. As we encounter the accoutrements of everyday life-perhaps a tree, for example-we might disregard the tree as unimportant or else begin to label it. Tree, conifer, blue pine. Needles, branches, trunk, roots, bark, top, cones. Part of the experience of awe is doing neither: neither disregarding nor disassembling the experience. To stand in awe of the tree (or any of the other wonders of daily life) is to encounter it as it really is, without the filters of priority or label. To smell it, notice its color, feel its various textures; to be in relationship to it (perhaps it towers overhead? Or shelters us from wind or sun?). This part of awe might be called wonderment. We approach the experience with neither questions nor answers, merely with openness to the experience.

A third component of awe might be respectfulness: to approach an experience-especially another being-without expectations, without the need for mastery. For example, in encountering a dolphin or whale, one notices how one must appear to the animal, how we are at a mutual boundary of environment but also of understanding (Pierson, 2009, p. 63), and how the encounter must be temporary. We do not need to master the animal or be mastered by it, only to share the encounter in this moment.

These ideas manifest in therapy: the dread inherent in being, the openness to the experience, and the lack of need for mastery. The patient arrives for therapy, and we wish to engage with them as best we can. Their problems seem significant and can overwhelm us, and yet no problem can be significant in the face of existential dread; we whirl along through the cosmos dead or alive. Thus we can take some perspective with regard to these problems, and not be subsumed by them.

One tries to meet the patient without preconceptions-diagnosis, prognosis, labels, expectations. You are depressed, one might think, and depressed people usually have this or that experience and respond thus and so to various treatments, and therefore you should behave in this manner or that. Taking an awe-filled position, we drop such worrisome thoughts and concentrate rather on the meeting of these people in this place, and the mutual experience of one another. We become curious about the subjective experience of the other-and that curiosity becomes the basis for a relationship.

Finally, with no need to master the person, we can abandon – to an extent – our needs for the person to get or be better. We can naively experience their own perspective, their need for however they feel in this moment. We can hold their intentions and desires and hopes as well as their current experience. The therapy-goer, then, can experience their own problems in a safe, undemanding space.

Related ideas can be found in Yalom (everyone faces the same ultimate concerns, the loan of life); Frankl (meaning); May (encounter, centrality of being); Satir (spirituality; connectedness and experiential learning); Whitaker (role fluidity, madness and trickiness, diagnosis); Minuchin (adaptability).

The Truth. Like Yalom, Schneider (2008) submits that The Truth may not be very important. He offers his diagram of the process as a useful roadmap to be revised as the territory is explored more thoroughly rather than a representation of some absolute truth to be adhered to in a dogmatic or zealous fashion. Conversely, he argues in the same volume that the pressure of post-modern thinking to adopt a relativistic or constructivist point of view might be counter-productive; so long as it is embodied and deliberative, taking a point of view and believing it is a needful and helpful part of psychotherapy.

Outcome research supports this position to an extent. That the practitioner believes in what they do seems to account for more outcome variance than what, specifically, the practitioner actually does (Norcross, 2008). An omniscient or ambient point of view would seem to limit one's ability to believe one is doing "the right thing," thus limiting one's effectiveness to a like degree.

Related ideas can be found in Yalom (interpretation; responsibility assumption); Frankl (freedom); May (the centrality of being); Whitaker (diagnosis); Laing (mental illness); Perls (the importance of subjective data), Minuchin (family myth and narrative).

Liberation. Schneider espouses EI therapy as a psychology of liberation. He suggests a six-tier structure for existence, with each tier enmeshed with the other tiers. Beginning with physical freedom (freedom from disability or restraints, etc.) and environmental freedom (e.g., freedom from toxins, noise, chaos) and proceeding to interpersonal and experiential freedom (such as to choose one's actions or assign meaning to objective events), he describes how people can experience their lives in a manner that is more or less free. He suggests that the ultimate goal of EI therapy is to help the person experience as much freedom as possible within the established boundaries.

Schneider goes on to suggest that, while the ideal goal might be experiential liberation, the reality of the therapy-goer's conditions might limit the degree of freedom that is truly available. Thus we might operate at a lower- or middle-level of liberation, such as cognitive freedom, because that is what is available and realistic for the therapy-goer. He suggests that this sort of work establishes "footholds on the toilsome path within" (2008, p. 51). This is to say, moving more towards physical freedom helps establish the basis for environmental freedom, and so on.

While Frankl argued that self-actualization is not impossible even in the face of missing blocks from the bottom of Maslow's pyramid, and even that the hopelessness of ever obtaining any of those missing blocks might concretize the need for self-actualization, it does not seem that Schneider disputes the attainability of experiential liberation in the face of lower-order concerns, or that attainment of other sorts of freedom is a prerequisite for experiential liberation; he maintains that there is permeability in the access to freedom (personal communication, Oct. 13, 2009.) Rather Frankl and Schneider seem to agree that these sorts of attainments ought not be ignored in the pure pursuit of self-actualization – that one ought not to suffer for the sake of it. Moreover, Schneider suggests that attaining lower-order freedoms helps put us on a path to attain the higher-order ones without ever suggesting that such attainments are necessary or sufficient.

Related ideas can be found in Yalom (responsibility assumption, everyone faces the same ultimate concerns, all problems are interpersonal problems, authenticity, the healing relationship, the loan of life); Frankl (meaning, freedom, happiness); May (will, angst, madness, anger and the Daimonic, intentionality, the centrality of being); Bowen (differentiation); Satir (shame vs. self-esteem); Whitaker (role fluidity, madness and trickiness); Minuchin (spontaneity); Perls (now I am aware…).

Invoking the Actual. Schneider (2008) refers to invoking the actual as the process of inviting and inspiring the therapy-goer to presence. Much as the therapist attempts to be present to the therapy-goer, so the therapy-goer can learn to be present to their self and their situations.

He suggests that the primary method of inspiring this presence is through presence (2008, pp. 62-65). That is, by staying present and inviting presence to the therapy-goer, the person is inspired to become more present (much like Yalom's axiom: disclosure begets disclosure).

Some other suggested methods for inspiring presence include: embodied meditation – a guided meditation centered on body-awareness; experimentation; and encounter between the therapist and the therapy-goer.

Related ideas can be found in Yalom (here and now focus and limited disclosure, healing relationship, authenticity); May (encounter, courage); Bowen (coaching); Satir (congruence, connectedness and experiential learning); Whitaker (symbolic experiential treatment, personal involvement, self-disclosure, using the self in therapy and doing one's own work); Minuchin (joining the system, experiential approach); Perls (look inside, look outside, now I am aware).

Vivifying and Confronting Resistance Self-Protections. This means, in short, helping people discover, close-up, how they resist and defend. Where Bugental (1981) suggested aligning with resistance, Schneider suggests more directly helping the therapy-goer experience the feelings and actions of their self-protections. What is the feeling in their body? What emotions or images come to mind? How can the person understand their resistance?

At a more direct level of encounter, for example, when there is a need to alarm, not just alert a client about how they keep themselves from a fuller self-encounter, one can help the therapy-goer confront their resistance. Confrontation over and above vivification is a particularly artful and delicate mode that should only be engaged with the utmost care and discernment (Schneider, personal communication, October 13, 2009). Schneider states the importance of not using I statements or interjecting material about the resistance; this can lead to reinforcing the resistance or, worse, capitulation on the part of the therapy-goer. Rather, he suggests bringing the person into confrontation with their own resistance, perhaps by asking strongly worded questions. For example, one might ask, "How long are you going to let your anger keep you from doing what you need to do?"

Related ideas can be found in Yalom (here and now focus and limited disclosure, healing relationship, authenticity); May (encounter, courage); Bowen (coaching); Satir (congruence, connectedness and experiential learning); Whitaker (symbolic experiential treatment, personal involvement, self-disclosure, using the self in therapy and doing one's own work); Minuchin (joining the system, experiential approach); Perls (look inside, look outside, now I am aware).

Constriction vs. Expansion. Along with liberation along these six dimensions, Schneider gives us a sort of unified Ultimate Concern. He suggests that we are continually faced with the choice (or at least the possibility) of extending or retracting when faced with the demands of being. Perhaps our confidence is challenged by an obstacle we have not faced before. We can choose to approach that obstacle with the belief that we are sufficient unto it, or retreat from it with the opposite belief.

These choices occur throughout the various levels of being: we can extend or retract visibly and physically; we can retreat from our surroundings or expand to occupy more of them with our bodies and possessions; we can come to dominate those around us or isolate from them; we can choose to choose our own path or choose passivity. We can also choose aimlessness or discipline, diffusion or focus, assertiveness or accommodation. This is the "fluid center" he refers to (Schneider, 2004, p. 11).

He posits that a certain amount of constriction and expansion is normal, healthy and natural. Perhaps a nine-foot high jump is not a normal progression from five; perhaps we are really not ready to move out of our parents' house at age 15. For the times when these growths or shrinkages, these extensions and retractions, are extreme and dysfunctional, he gives us the words hyperconstriction and hyperexpansion (Schneider ,1993). It is constrictive, for example, to shrink in fear from a person who poses an overt threat. It is hyperconstrictive to shrink from every person regardless of objective threat. It is expansive to apply for a job – or as many jobs as one can. It is most likely hyperexpansive to apply to be President of the United States.

Related ideas can be found in Yalom (we all face the same ultimate concerns); May (courage); Frankl (meaning); Laing (mental illness).

Paradox. Schneider notes paradoxes many times in his work; they are an ongoing and central theme. For example, he cites The *Incredible Shrinking Man* as an example of hyperconstriction (1993). The dread of becoming smaller and smaller is juxtaposed with the horror of the limitlessness of that smallness. He does not shrink to a definite size and then stop shrinking; his size becomes more and more bounded without a boundary to that boundedness. Ultimately, his shrinking seems to become a sort of diffusion – his ultimate smallness is that he merges into the background of the universe, becoming – horrifically –infinitesimal (Schneider, 1993).

Note Schneider's previous thought experiment about being both face-to-face with a person and yet also stuck on the world during part of its journey through the cosmos. To be with both experiences simultaneously is to invoke a feeling of awe.

This encounter with our ultimate smallness must necessarily also be an encounter with our ultimate unboundedness, or groundlessness. As the cosmos seems to be infinite, so must each divisible part of the cosmos be infinite (infinity divided by any number is infinity). Thus as one tries to break a person down into component parts, one finds one can never discover the smallest components. Muscles and bones yield molecules, which in turn surrender atoms. Atoms give us their nuclear components – positrons, neutrons, electrons. The atom is mostly empty space, reminiscent of contemplating the world in its lonely journey around the sun and through the vastness of the void. And the atom, when smashed, yields quarks, strangely non-massive, unspecific particles that relate only dimly with the background of the universe, perhaps as small in relation to us as we are in relation to the Milky Way galaxy. Finally, one might wonder whether it is reasonable to conclude that these subatomic scales are the end of the line or whether even more bizarre and exotic scales of being exist beneath quarks.

Paradoxically, we are tiny when faced with infinity – but also infinite in scale as we examine the microscales beneath us as well as the macroscales of which we are a part. We last an imperceptibly short time compared with the infinity of the expanding universe – but an immeasurably huge time next to the sorts of timescales inherent in the observation of subatomic particles.

Schneider (2008) seems to suggest there is some wisdom inherent in being able to consider both poles of an experience at one time–that which he also refers to as our capacity to be both fluid and centered. That two things that seem disparate might be true at once – our infinite smallness and our unimaginable hugeness at once – seems to be a key to the experience of awe. Schneider is silent on exactly how; he only points the way.

Meaning. Schneider (2008) suggests that meaning, a central facet in Existential theory, is composed of awe and intentionality, which in turn derive from a "whole-bodied" experience of freedom—freedom gained from the hard-won encounter with one's resistances. Through whole-bodied discovery, then, Experiential liberation allows the therapy-goer to engage with a sense of purposefulness in action. This purposefulness, this striving towards some long-term goal (perhaps as apparently mundane as weight loss or as evidently esoteric as spiritual growth) is intentionality, or meaningful engagement. This meaningful engagement in the context of awe-filled awareness forms the basis for meaning.

This theory of meaning is dissimilar to Frankl's concept of logotherapy inasmuch as meaning is not a post-hoc construction tacked onto a prior event (as for example in Frankl's case of a husband predeceased by his wife; Frankl asks the man to wonder how she would have felt had he died before her, and the husband comes to understand the meaning of his suffering was to spare his wife that same suffering Frankl, 2006, p.154). Rather, it is a way of engaging with the present and with one's own will in order that each moment is meaningful.

Frankl is sometimes criticized for this simple assignment of meaning (see for example Yalom, 1980, p. 470) but, while his techniques for helping the patient acquire meaning may seem facile, his understanding of the need for meaning is much deeper. With this in mind, Schneider's concept of meaning does not represent a direct argument with other concepts of meaning but an evolution in psychotherapeutic strategy to help evoke the person's own inherent sense of purpose.

For Schneider, Awe and Meaning are intertwined concepts; neither synonymous nor fully free of one another. While Awe on one hand provides a context for encounter and the development of a sense of Meaning, Awe can also be the outcome of such engagements. Full experiential liberation as culminating in a sense of humility and wonder, a reverent stance towards life and one's own life, becomes a core feature of EI Psychotherapy.

Related ideas can be found in Yalom (we all face the same ultimate concerns); Frankl (meaning); May (will, angst, intentionality); Satir (spirituality); Minuchin (family myth and narrative); Laing (mental illness); Perls (the importance of subjective data).

Victor Frankl

Frankl was a psychiatrist in Vienna prior to the outbreak of World War II (WWII) and had already begun writing on the subject of Logotherapy. During his internment, one of his main concerns was his ability to recreate the manuscripts he had lost at the time of his imprisonment. He did eventually recreate and add to his work on Logotherapy.

In terms of the question of Existentialism, however, his many volumes of literature are rarely mentioned. Rather, *Man's Search for Meaning* remains the centerpiece of his contribution to Existential thought, and thus is the work under major consideration here.

Meaning. Frankl's (2006) seminal title, *Man's Search for Meaning*, is concerned almost singularly with the concept of meaning. Frankl describes his life in WWII concentration camps as an allegory for lives in which suffering is inevitable. He posits also that suffering is relative: "Thus suffering completely fills the human soul and conscious mind, no matter whether the suffering is great or little. Therefore the "size" of suffering is always relative" (p. 44). His primary thesis is that those who were able to cling to some sort of meaning were more likely to survive than those for whom there was no meaning in their experience.

Frankl (2006) divides meaning into three component parts: the creation of a work or a deed; an encounter with someone or experience with some thing; and one's stance towards unavoidable suffering. This idea dominates his thinking and writing: that meaning in life is ultimately found in the way we confront what we cannot control. For example:

> Dostoevsky said once, 'There is only one thing that I dread: to not be worthy of my sufferings.' These words frequently came to my mind after I became aware of those martyrs whose behavior in camp, whose suffering and death, bore witness to the fact that the last inner freedom cannot be lost. It can be said that they were worthy of their sufferings; the way they bore their suffering was a genuine inner achievement. It is this spiritual freedom – which cannot be taken away – that makes life meaningful and purposeful. (p. 66)

And:

> "Suffering had become a task on which we did not want to turn our backs. We had realized its hidden opportunities for achievement, the opportunities which caused Rilke to write, 'Wie viel ist aufzuleiden!' (How much suffering there is to get through!) Rilke spoke of 'getting through suffering' as others would talk of 'getting through work.' There was plenty of suffering for us to get through. Therefore, it was necessary to face up to the full amount of suffering, trying o keep moments of weakness and furtive tears to a minimum. But there was no

need to be ashamed of tears, for tears bore witness that a man had the greatest of courage, the courage to suffer." (p. 77)

Related ideas can be found in Yalom (we all face the same ultimate concerns, responsibility assumption, the loan of life, interpretation, the healing relationship, authenticity); Schneider (awe, liberation); May (encounter, courage, intentionality, the centrality of being); Satir (congruence, spirituality); Minuchin (adaptability, family myth and narrative); Perls (encounter).

Freedom. Frankl (2006) writes: "…everything can be taken from man but one thing: the last of the human freedoms – the freedom to choose one's attitude in any given set of circumstances, to choose one's way" (p. 66). This sentiment is restated a number of times in a number of ways, that this last of the human freedoms is really central to the human condition. A focus of Frankl's work was to help people become liberated from circumstance.

Part of liberation from circumstance is acceptance of responsibility. The freedom to choose one's way is also the responsibility to do so. Life owes us nothing, but perhaps we owe something to life.

Related ideas can be found in Yalom (we all face the same ultimate concerns, responsibility assumption); Schneider (liberation); May (courage, will, angst, anxiety, intentionality); Bowen (differentiation); Satir (congruence, freedom and responsibility); Whitaker (role fluidity, madness and trickiness); Minuchin (the rules, adaptability).

Happiness. For Frankl, happiness is not a goal for psychotherapy. Paradoxically, this makes happiness an expected outcome. He writes: "Happiness must happen… you have to let it happen by not caring about it." And: "for success, like happiness, cannot be pursued; it must ensue…" (2006, p. xiv).

Thus happiness is the consequence of a life lived well, not a goal to strive for. One is happy when one lives according to one's values and takes responsibility for one's actions. Thus: "…there could be no earthly happiness that could compensate for all we had suffered. We were not hoping for happiness – it was not that which gave us courage and gave meaning to our suffering, our sacrifices and our dying" (p. 92).

Related ideas can be found in Yalom (we all face the same ultimate concerns); Schneider (awe).

Rollo May

Rollo May is widely credited with bringing Existentialism from Europe to the United States. His own training was in Psychoanalysis; May notes that he learned about Existentialism largely during his confinement in a care center for tuberculosis, each day unsure if he would live another day.

His writings span decades and cover art, Greek philosophy and religion, anxiety, love, will, and a multitude of other subjects.

Courage. Rollo May was influenced substantially by Paul Tillich, whose writings on theology form a basis for much of modern existential thought. In particular, May's (1994) descriptions of courage as taking place in several contexts (the courage to suffer, physical courage, moral courage, and social courage) draw heavily on Tillich's influence.

Suffering. "…courage is not the absence of despair; it is, rather, the capacity to move ahead *in spite of despair*" (p. 8, italics in original). Thus, like Frankl, May advocates a sort of courage in which the way we deal with inescapable suffering is more important than whether we survive another minute or another day. Virtue and meaning are found in the actions we take in the face of inevitability.

The concepts introduced by May are all interlocked. Will enters this equation as a form of choicefulness: one can choose one's responses to adverse circumstances. This concept is intensely important to psychotherapy, inasmuch as the psychotherapist can rarely (if ever) do anything to ameliorate the suffering of a patient by the means of altering their situation or circumstances. Rather, the psychotherapist must help the patient to discover their will through their choicefulness, even at times when the person seems to be or feels unfree.

Physical courage. "The use of the body… for the cultivation of sensitivity" (1994, p. 15). That is, rather than antiquated notions of heroism based on athleticism or victory in battle, May implies a movement towards attunement with our bodies, towards thinking more physically. Thus we can come to know the other by our body's reaction to him.

May saw American culture as a collection of people becoming increasingly disconnected from one another and from their selves. Here he is advocating a re-engagement with the other through re-engagement with the self. Physical courage is choosing to feel something visceral for and about other people, even though these feelings will make us somehow more responsible.

Freedom is more clearly visible in the presence of knowledge. Feeling something for or about somebody provides a person with more information and, thereby, more responsibility (freedom). It would seem easier to open one's laptop on the train or close one's eyes and listen to one's favorite music on the IPOD than to look our fellow strangers in the eye and feel something deeply for them.

Moral courage. By this, May means the way we commit to a belief and are willing to defend it. Openly declaring one is willing to perform abortions because one believes in women's right to choose is a form of moral courage when social pressure (up to and including murder) is present to declare the opposite.

In the moment, it may be difficult to stand up for something one believes in deeply because there are pressures in the moment contrary to that belief. Take, for example, peer or social pressure, filial pressure, or the needs for safety or sustenance. Standing up for the biblical Ten Commandments when one is a Supreme Court Justice might not be a very good career move. Standing for the right to suicide might be a bad idea for a medical doctor.

Moral beliefs often take a back seat to the more pragmatic needs of the moment. Moral courage means putting these beliefs in the driver's seat when doing so presents some form of risk to the individual.

Social courage. By this, May means letting ourselves see the suffering of other people, thus experiencing evil and being forced to take a stand (one way or another). Additionally, he means relating to others in a way that demands increasing intimacy, openness, and risk. The uncourageous thing to do, conversely, would be to become blind to the suffering of others, and to the effect one has upon others. Without ever being really confronted by empathy or sympathy, by remaining forever enclosed within the fortress of our defenses, one need never take a stand or become responsible.

Here again May gives us knowledge as a component of will. As in physical courage, social courage means exposing oneself to knowledge upon which one might have to act in order to maintain a positive self-image. One might ignore a beggar and pretend not to have seen him rather than face the guilt of deciding, with full and obvious knowledge of the plight of the other, not to be of service.

This may be another of May's comments on the moral dissolution present in American society: people simply do not seem to care about one another. Moreover, people are essentially good (a comment with which May himself might be inclined to argue, but which is implied here) and, were they to allow themselves to be aware of the suffering of others, would be compelled to care and thus responsible to help.

As the person must be both the one who is tricked into not seeing and the one tricking, however, the responsibility is ultimately unavoidable. Freedom cannot be given away no matter how hard one tries.

Related ideas can be found in Frankl (meaning, freedom); Schneider (meaning); Bowen (differentiation); Satir (congruence, freedom and responsibility); Whitaker (using the self in therapy and doing one's own work, personal involvement); Minuchin (joining the system); Perls (encounter).

Will. Care is the opposite of apathy. What is required is that we care about something. Lacking care, we lack also will; lacking will we lack the capacity to wish. An uncaring life is an apathetic life, devoid of meaning and satisfaction (May, 1969).

Will is the thing that not only enables us to pursue and enact our wishes, but the thing that allows us to wish in the first place. Thus before we have a will to power, we must have a will to will. Our freedom is ultimately inescapable; handing over our freedom to another entity is itself an act of will; a free person can deny their own freedom precisely because it is free (1969, 1983).

An aspect of will, intentionality, is the purposefulness of a person, the drive to do actively rather than be acted upon passively. The meaningfulness of life centers in the purposefulness of a person they strive and contend with life (May, 1989).

Related ideas can be found in Yalom (we all face the same ultimate concerns, responsibility assumption); Schneider (liberation, vivifying and confronting resistances and self-protections); Frankl (freedom); Bowen (differentiation); Satir (congruence); Whitaker (using the self in therapy and doing one's own work, directiveness); Minuchin (the rules); Perls (encounter).

Angst. Angst is a sort of responsibility. It is an awakening to the fact that one risks annihilation as long as one escapes it; anxiety, then, is rooted in our being. Anxiety is not something that we have or experience; it is something that we are.

Humanity, says May (1969), is the thing that is aware of its own existence and that can take responsibility for this existence. It is unclear whether a dog, for example, knows that it exists. It is clear that a person knows they exist and wish this condition to continue.

Furthermore, people are the only being that can take (or abdicate) responsibility for the conditions of their existence, including its internal experiences and freedoms.

For May, this knowledge is the source of freedom (and responsibility). While angst and responsibility seem disparate at first reading, they grow closer in definition the more they are considered (May, 1969).

Related ideas can be found in Yalom (we all face the same ultimate concerns, responsibility assumption); Schneider (liberation); Frankl (freedom); Bowen (differentiation); Satir (congruence); Whitaker (role fluidity, madness and trickiness); Minuchin (the rules, adaptability).

Anxiety. Anxiety is part of the human condition, May contends. It is not a disease to be cured or an obstacle to be conquered; rather, it is an intrinsic part of being human. An anxiety-free existence would be an inhuman existence, absent of the motivation to accomplish anything.

School papers are written out of anxiety; from such modest beginnings as the flutter in one's stomach when one contemplates one's own headstone are born the world's great monuments. May, then, does not seek to annihilate anxiety (which would be tantamount to annihilating the person) but to channel it into productive venues (May, 1950/1996).

He compares anxiety to the creative urge, for example, and shows us how artistic expression is impossible without it. Indeed, he finds art to be a way free of the torment of anxiety while leaving anxiety intact (May, 1994).

Related ideas can be found in Schneider (invoking the actual).

Encounter. We can love, despite the fact that love ends inevitably in loss: either we or the object of our affections must leave the earth (May, 1994). For May, this is the highest form of healing. Angst, care, will and courage all culminate in a meeting between people that is creative and engaging. Through this encounter with the other, the very things needed to make the encounter possible are strengthened.

The authentic engagement does not require that one take a one-up or one-down position. Thus the will is bolstered, nurtured, shown love. A one-up encounter shows fear for will, and a one-down shows repression of it; engagement shows care. Angst is a given; the encounter must end, the person must end, annihilation is inevitable – and yet we engage regardless (or regardfully). We are responsible to do so precisely because we will soon be gone, precisely because it is now that we are here. Courage, too, is bolstered as our boldness is rewarded with being seen, and with seeing. And to see the other is to care for the other – and to be cared for.

Related ideas can be found in Yalom (we all face the same ultimate concerns, authenticity, the healing relationship, here and now orientation and limited disclosure); Schneider (awe, liberation, meaning); Frankl (meaning); Bowen (coaching, societal emotional process); Satir (connectedness and experiential learning); Whitaker (limited encounter, symbolic experiential treatment); Minuchin (joining the system, experiential approach); Perls (look inside, look outside, now I am aware…).

The Daimonic. May invokes the idea of the Daimonic, hinting at an elucidation of Jung's *Shadow*. For May, the Daimonic is a force within the personality that is untended. It can be positive or negative, good or evil, but it is denied or invisible to the person it inhabits. And, so long as it remains invisible or denied, it has the power to dominate the personality.

As such, one powerful way of coping with the Daimonic is naming. May (1969) suggests that, as demons cowered from the sound of their own names, so too the Daimonic shrinks to a manageable size when confronted with direct attention, with its own name.

Related ideas can be found in Schneider (vivifying and confronting resistances and self protections).

The centrality of being. Descartes said, "Cognito, ergo sum." May (1983), however, contends that thinking is meaningless without first being; the fact of existence is obvious and does not require thought as proof. This contention is seen in his criticisms of Psychoanalysis that seeks after transference and repression; without being in this moment in this place, no transference is possible. It is being in this moment that makes possible all of the convolutions associated with Psychoanalysis.

Throughout *The Discovery of Being* (1983) he urges us to do whatever is necessary to shine light upon the being of the patient in the moment, to reveal what it is possible to reveal about the person as they exist now, to see them and reflect that sight into their own eyes.

Related ideas can be found in Yalom (we all face the same ultimate concerns); Schneider (awe).

Myth. May (1991) frequently cites myth as central to understanding the human condition, and frequently used Greek mythology to illustrate his own search for meaning, intentionality, courage, will, and so on. He offered myth as a sort of guiding narrative in order to help makes sense out of lives that are becoming increasingly valueless and nihilistic.

Related ideas can be found in Minuchin (family myth and narrative); Whitaker (myth).

Murray Bowen

Bowen was a psychiatrist and a family systems researcher and practitioner. The body of his literature is mostly journal articles and book chapters; he also exerted influence as the first president of the American Family Therapy Association (AFTA).

Coaching. Murray presented the idea of a non-standard therapeutic relationship in which the patients (family members) learned about functional behaviors by practicing them and by the therapist embodying them (especially differentiation, below). Behaving in a rational manner, aware of one's role and function, became a habit that increased differentiation and functionality (Crown, Freeman & Freeman, 1993).

Related ideas can be found in Schneider (invoking the actual); Satir (congruence, the monad); Whitaker (using the self in therapy and doing one's own work, directiveness, limited encounter).

Differentiation. This idea is similar to individuation. It refers to a person's ability to think, feel and act separate from one's family. The differentiated person feels like a complete person, grounded in a well-established selfhood; this selfhood allows relationships (particularly filial relationships) characterized by rationality rather than susceptibility to emotional pressure (Bowen, 1992). Such a person makes decisions, has thoughts and beliefs, and takes actions that are all in accordance with one another.

Later, the term 'enmeshment' would come into popular use; while Bowen (1992) did not speak of enmeshment, differentiation can be thought of as the light that makes this darkness visible. The undifferentiated person does not have an internal reservoir of approval and must seek it from their family, either through servile or authoritarian behavior. Rather than being rational, the undifferentiated person behaves (thinks, makes decisions, and takes actions) not in such a way that these things match, but in such a way as to meet the need for external approval.

Related ideas can be found in Schneider (vivifying and confronting resistances and self protections; May (courage, will, encounter, The Daimonic, intentionality); Satir (congruence, Chaos vs. homeostasis, self-esteem vs. shame, freedom and responsibility); Whitaker (co-therapy, role-fluidity, use of self in therapy and doing one's own work); Perls (encounter).

Triangles. Triangles (later known as 'triangulation') are a way of diminishing anxiety within a dyad. When one relationship is in conflict, each member of the dyad resorts to relating to another person outside the dyad. This might be in order to "win" the conflict by getting the new addition to take one's side, though most often the conflict is avoided. Each party might take on a new relationship (or project facets of the conflicted relationship onto an existing one) separately, such that the triangle really has four (or even more) points (Bowen, 1992).

A healthy system would be characterized by each party dealing with its conflicts directly rather than through triangulated systems.

Related ideas can be found in Yalom (authenticity, the healing relationship); Schneider (invoking the actual, vivifying and confronting resistances and self protections); May (courage, encounter); Satir (congruence, the monad, self-esteem vs. shame, connectedness and experiential learning); Whitaker (symbolic experiential therapy, triangulation); Minuchin (diagrams, rules); Laing (mental illness); Perls (encounter).

Emotional Cutoff. This term refers to a divorce of emotions, sometimes relating to others and sometimes to oneself. Unable or unwilling to tolerate the anxiety present in family interactions, a family member becomes distant or isolated. This can occur by spending too much time at work or out of the house with friends, by moving away and visiting rarely, as well as by remaining physically present to the family but reserved and reticent.

The cure for emotional cutoff according to Bowen is increasing extended family relationships and working on openness. The cutoff occurs in order to avoid the anxiety present in the family system. However, that anxiety and the situation it refers to are never actually dealt with or processed; thus the need to maintain the cutoff remains in place indefinitely. Working on openness offers the potential to process the initial conflict or anxiety-producing dynamic, thereby reducing or eliminating the need for cutoff (Bowen, 1992).

Related ideas can be found in Yalom (we all face the same ultimate concerns: authenticity, the healing relationship, here and now orientation and limited disclosure); Schneider (awe, liberation, meaning); Frankl (meaning); May (encounter, courage, will); Satir (connectedness and experiential learning); Whitaker (limited encounter, symbolic experiential treatment); Minuchin (joining the system, experiential approach); Perls (look inside, look outside, now I am aware…).

Nuclear Family Emotional System. Long-standing tension, especially if it is severe, can result in various family problems. The problems come about as a result of the triangulation or cutoff used to cope with the anxiety created by the tension. Dyads can become dysfunctional (especially the parental couple); an over-accommodating family member can appear ill; a child can fail to differentiate.

The anxiety eventually finds a home in one or more individuals or relationships within the family. Bowen posits a finite amount of anxiety with certain parts of the family doing a disproportionate share of the coping. Over a long period of time, this can result in severe psychopathology, social problems, or medical issues (Bowen, 1992).

Related ideas can be found in Laing (mental illness); Satir (shame vs. self-esteem).

Family Projection Process. Parents hand down their coping behaviors to their children, as well as their emotional difficulties. An over-anxious couple, for example, might teach the child both to be anxious much of the time and to cope with that anxiety in dysfunctional ways.

Bowen suggests a three-stage process for fostering this sort of multi-generational transmission of emotional problems. First, the parents think there is something wrong with the child; next, they confirm their suspicions through observation (whether or not they are actually correct); last, they treat the child in a manner consistent with the imagined problem.

This can result in creating the problem one fears. For example, a child perceived as needy receives rejection in order to train self-reliance; that rejection creates low self-efficacy and the need to seek approval externally (Bowen, 1992).

Related ideas can be found in Laing (mental illness); Satir (shame vs. self-esteem).

Societal Emotional Process. This is the idea that certain types of social institutions function much like family systems. For example, courts might have a sort of parental authority, and the way they hand down judgments might affect people (especially children) much as parental judgments impact development. A court that is unreasonably harsh, for example, becomes the authoritarian parent; ultimately, it teaches that power is good and being in control is good. The overt message (which might be, "comply with the law") is subsumed by the covert message, and the use of power is learned directly through observing the use of power.

Places of employment, schools, self-help groups, chess clubs, and any other time three or more people are present in one place potentially include Family Systems dynamics (Bowen, 1992).

Related ideas can be found in Laing (mental illness); Satir (shame vs. self-esteem).

Virginia Satir

One of the most influential practitioners and theorists in Family Systems Therapy, Satir wrote more than a dozen books on topics from authenticity to child-rearing. Her theories have valance not only in family therapy but also in organizational psychology and institutes dedicated to Satir and her work can be found worldwide. This dissertation will deal primarily with her work on family systems.

Congruence. Satir wrote frequently about the idea of congruence (for example, Baldwin, 1999). Similar to the ideas of presence and authenticity, what she means by congruence is that one's thoughts match one's stated beliefs, intentions, and behavior. A parent who tells the child not to hit and spanks the child for hitting is incongruent; their stated belief in not hitting is belied by the action of spanking. Thus the child does not learn not to hit; the child learns, perhaps, not to hit in sight of the parent, or to only hit if the child is bigger and stronger than whomever they want to hit.

Her approach to therapy consisted largely of behaving in a congruent manner and pointing out incongruence. While she was dedicated to certain values (such as peace and non-violence; see for example Satir, 1988), she mostly aimed to help people act according to their beliefs and convey covert messages that did not contradict their overt messages. Baldwin (1999) says of congruence:

> One of the basic qualities necessary to be "more fully human" is congruence. Congruence is the ability to see and say things as they are, while respecting the Self, the Other and the Context. This is an essential quality the therapist needs to make wise and honest decisions regarding the use of self with another person in a given context. In the state of congruence, the self of the therapist is fully present, nondefensive and thus vulnerable, aware of the needs, vulnerabilities and possible defenses of the other, within the context of the situation, in this case the therapeutic situation. (p. xxii)

The concept of Congruence must also include metacommunication, that which is communicated beyond the intended communication. When one says one thing but behaves differently, one communicates both the behavior and the dishonesty as well as the stated communication. The art of being Congruent does not stamp out metacommunication, but does make the metacommunications consistent with the primary communications, increasing the power of the message conveyed.

When communication contains respect for self, other and context, the metacommunications will likely fall in line with the primary communication. If this respect is missing at one or more levels, it sets up systemic stress which must be coped with. Incongruent coping styles fall into a few basic patterns (Satir, 1988): blaming, with which one intends to avoid responsibility for a problem by making someone else feel that responsibility; placating, which is an attempt to avoid the stress of confrontation by taking the blame; irrelevance, which is little more than changing the subject away from issues that are stressful; and being super-reasonable (the Computer), which means closing out affect completely and doing only what makes logical sense.

Each of these coping patterns has benefits (mostly avoiding the stress inherent in the incongruent communication) and drawbacks (mostly making another person responsible for most of the coping; see Bowen, above, for the consequences of individuals doing a disproportionate share of coping in a system).

Related ideas can be found in Yalom (authenticity, the healing relationship, here and now orientation and limited disclosure); Schneider (invoking the actual, vivifying and confront resistances and self-protections); May (courage, The Daimonic); Bowen (triangles); Whitaker (use of self in therapy and doing your own work, personal involvement); Minuchin (read this book and forget about it); Laing (mental illness).

The Monad. By this Satir means the self, the individual. She noted the importance of doing one's own work first; no dyad can be functional if one of the monads is dysfunctional. The relationship must compensate. Furthermore, the therapeutic relationship must accommodate the unwise therapist, who is in danger of getting sucked into the dysfunctional systems that present.

Thus Satir recommended a firm grounding through meditation, therapy, contemplation, introspection, and whatever else helps one become a more distinct self. Knowing one's own values as well as being grounded in a sense of self-esteem and self-acceptance makes it possible to be with another person in a constructive fashion, without the danger of seeking to gratify one's own needs through the therapeutic relationship. (Baldwin, 1999; Satir et al., 1991).

This stance also includes the use of self in therapy, including self disclosure and joining the system. A strong alliance requires the willingness to refuse a superordinate position and her experiential focus implies working change from within the system. Additionally, she advocated intuition, or using one's own feelings about people and their relationships in therapy: the work on the monad is crucial to this perspective on healing. This human validation process model (Satir & Bitter, 2000) values the relationship of the therapist with the family over any sort of techniques and is a source of Satir's reputation as a humanist.

Related ideas can be found in Schneider (awe, invoking the actual); May (courage); Whitaker (using the self in therapy and doing one's own work); Minuchin (joining the system; experiential approach); Perls (look inside, look outside).

Chaos vs. homeostasis. Satir (1991) betrays an interest in operant conditioning with the concept of Chaos. In Chaos, one or more members of a system have begun to change the way they react to others. Other members of the system expect a predictable reaction when they behave in a certain way and do not receive that reaction; thus they try again and more forcefully to elicit the expected reaction. The phenomenon of Chaos can be described as the system trying to regain homeostatis, pressuring members to not change, to return to the baseline function. At this homeostatic baseline, behaviors are met with predictable responses, sameness is perpetuated, and the system is comfortable (even if dysfunctional). It may be that systems prefer homeostasis to functionality; change is a sort of stress because, at an operant conditioning level, it creates chaos even if it results in individuals getting what they desire.

Chaos is also responsible for the phenomenon of dysfunction growing worse before it grows better. Families can expect to see their problems temporarily exacerbated as the system and its members have to unlearn old ways of getting their needs met and learn new ways.

Spirituality. Satir described her work as more spiritual than clinical; numerous authors have contended that it was her deep belief that all humans are wonderful beings that was her major contribution in family therapy (Brothers, 1991). As seen above, she espoused a contemplative lifestyle and believed in the core values of peacefulness and congruence. She wrote extensively about non-aggression, meaning not only non-violence but also abandoning the need to control other people, stating that the congruent, self-esteeming person does not need to be forceful or authoritarian. She particularly espoused this stance in dealing with children, who perhaps would get better treatment if they were not born so small (Baldwin, 1999; Satir, 1991).

Satir had larger concerns than solving family problems. She stated that she was healing the world a little bit each time she helped a family to heal; the world, after all, is composed of families. This was a moral mission, a spiritual endeavor, and never a matter of mere clinical significance (Brothers, 1991).

Related ideas can be found in Schneider (awe); Minuchin (family myth and narrative); Whiter (Myth).

Self-esteem vs. Shame. In raising children, parents always affect the conflict between shame and self-esteem. By behaving in a disapproving or authoritarian manner, we increase shame; by behaving in a loving, teaching manner, we increase self-esteem.

Satir (1988) contended that there are many–mostly covert–ways in which families drive their children towards the shame side of the balance. She also believed in triads: relationships between three individuals in which feelings towards one member are displaced onto another. Shame often comes from these triadic displacements.

The cure for the creation of shame is congruence, as described above.

Related ideas can be found in Bowen (triangulation).

Connectedness and experiential learning. Satir believed in creating encounter, that people learned about relating to others by being related to by others. Metaphysically, she referenced a sort of enmeshment of being, a cosmic intertwinement, but clinically she meant that the therapeutic relationship was a thing of healing.

Related topics are the use of self in therapy and congruence. These core ideas contributed to the connectedness between the therapist and the members of the family, and helped teach that connectedness between members of the family (Satir, 1988).

Related ideas can be found in Yalom (we all face the same ultimate concerns, authenticity, the healing relationship, here and now orientation and limited disclosure); Schneider (awe, liberation, meaning); Frankl (meaning); May (encounter); Bowen (coaching, societal emotional process); Whitaker (limited encounter, symbolic experiential treatment); Minuchin (joining the system, experiential approach); Perls (look inside, look outside, now I am aware…).

Freedom and responsibility. Satir made few direct remarks about the Existential givens. Her work does have many connections, particularly her stance on congruence and coping; becoming more conscious of the way one copes with stress and communicates makes one more responsible for one's coping and communication.

She does speak directly to the idea of freedom and responsibility in her five freedoms (Satir, 1995). They are: to see and hear what is here, instead of what should be, was, or will be; to say what one feels and thinks instead of what one should; to feel what one feels, instead of what one ought; to ask for what one wants, instead of always waiting for permission; and to take risks in [sic] one's own behalf, instead of choosing to be only "secure" and not rocking the boat.

It is of note that each of these freedoms implies a responsibility; if one is free to respond to the world as it is rather than as it should be, the implication is that one has until now been responding to an imaginary world. The freedom to say what one thinks rather than what one should say implies a responsibility to be honest. To feel one's own feelings rather than repressing them out of social nicety implies one is responsible for what one feels (whether repressed or not). The freedom to ask for what one wants implies one is responsible for doing so; unmet needs become the product of passivity. The freedom to take risks implies perhaps the most terrifying responsibility of all.

Related ideas can be found in Yalom (we all face the same ultimate concerns; responsibility assumption); Schneider (liberation, vivifying and confronting resistances and self-protections, paradox, meaning, constriction vs. expansion); Frankl (meaning, freedom); May (courage, angst, anxiety, will); Whitaker (family life cycle, givens of family existence, myth); Minuchin (family life cycle, family myth and narrative).

Rules. Like Whitaker and Minuchin (below), Satir believes rules are necessary in a system and best when flexible. Excessively rigid rules as well as absent or excessively inconsistent rules are signs of dysfunction in a system (1988, p. 5). Rules and roles are a blended concept; Satir insists that people must have the ability, as well as the freedom, to behave in ways that are honest, spontaneous and respectful, rather than rigid and predetermined.

Pathology. The main measure of pathology for Satir is self-esteem. As communication moves away from congruence, metacommunication results in double-binds (one cannot obey both the explicit and covert message;, therefore, one must accept anxiety). As double-binds accrue, a person repeatedly fails at the tasks set by the family system and thereby loses self-esteem. Low self esteem causes the maladaptive coping strategies outlined above as well as conflicted metacommunication, which keeps the whole system working to reduce the self-esteem of its members.

A person with high self esteem has no need to avoid anxieties such as blame or the negative affect of others (see "the monad" above). Thus the high self esteem person can deal directly with the source of conflict, avoiding triangulation, and can do so congruently, avoiding conflicted metacommunication (1988, p. 5).

This leaves Satir with two basic ways to help cure pathology in a system: either deal directly with the issue of congruence and communication patterns, or deal directly with the issue of self esteem. Satir's methods for doing therapy generally place a heavy emphasis on dealing with the communications issues explicitly and overtly; however, her philosophic work emphasizes the value of each person and her belief that every human being is wonderful. Much as the Existentialist adopts a contemplative lifestyle in order to be of better service to others (see Schneider's "awe" above, for example) Satir adopts a stance of lovingness and wonder for each person that is intrinsically healing and that transcends techniques.

Spontaneity as Authenticity. Satir (1983) states that her theories and techniques are not the best or only way of doing things, and insists that therapists retain their own flavor, or way of doing things. Their mannerisms and personality are an important part of the package; that is, their essential humanity and healing nature ought not be sacrificed to the idea of technique.

(Related ideas can be found in Yalom (interpretation); Schneider (invoking the actual); May (read this book and forget about it); Whitaker (craziness and trickiness).

Carl Whitaker

Whitaker practiced as a Family Systems Therapist following experiences working with psychotic individuals and with children. The spontaneous, confrontational style he developed in these settings was infamous. He contended for years that this style could not effectively be taught or written about, but only learned via experience.

Co-therapy. Whitaker was a pioneer in the idea of co-therapy: using more than one therapist. The advantages of a co-therapy approach in Systemic work are many, including: the ability for one therapist to make process comments regarding the interaction of the other therapist with the family; the ability to model appropriate conflict between therapists; the ability to effect longer and more productive transitions and transfers; the ability to focus the attention of one therapist while maintaining a more diffuse attention from the other.

These advantages are played out in dramatic fashion in *The Family Crucible* (Napier and Whitaker, 1978),when a here-and-now process focus under the eyes and guidance of two therapists helped destabilize a family in therapy, moving them away from their rigid and dysfunctional patterns towards more choiceful behavior.

Napier and Whitaker characterize their co-therapy in this book as symbolic of a marriage; the whole family becomes their children in this metaphor, and as they discuss their treatment options with one another, they help the real parents experience thoughtful parenting. This vignette helps illustrate Whitaker's overarching theory of Symbolic Experiential treatment.

Related ideas can be found in May (will); Schneider (invoking the actual); Perls (now I am aware).

Symbolic Experiential Treatment. Whitaker (1981) contends that most of the progress a family will make in therapy is due to processes that are covert and non-verbal. While many therapists strive to make the unconscious conscious, it is Whitaker's position that this is neither necessary nor sufficient. Process is learned by process, he suggests, and talking about process is useful only inasmuch as it models a sort of process.

He suggests that families prefer stability (homeostasis) to functionality; something that does not work will be repeated endlessly simply because that is what people are used to doing. The process of Symbolic Experiential therapy, then, is one of introducing new ways of behaving that are unbalancing, destabilizing. The destabilized family is one that is moved away from homeostasis by the therapist entering into the system and behaving in a novel (often provocative) fashion.

Little or nothing is learned in this process, at least at a cognitive, verbal, explicit level. Rather, due to the new stimulus (a provocative therapist), the family is forced to behave in novel ways rather than in the homeostatic fashion that is the problem.

Related ideas can be found in Yalom (we all face the same ultimate concerns, authenticity, the healing relationship, here and now orientation and limited disclosure); Schneider (awe, liberation, meaning); Frankl (meaning); May (encounter); Bowen (coaching, societal emotional process); Satir (connectedness and experiential learning); Minuchin (joining the system, experiential approach); Perls (look inside, look outside, now I am aware…).

Personal involvement. *The Family Crucible* illustrates that Whitaker (1978) becomes personally involved with his families. It is his own personal growth and change that he sees as the change agent rather than cognitive realizations or insight. Thus he uses his charisma to join the system without being overpowered by it, aligns with the system, and trusts that his own presence is enough to effect change. He rarely actually wrote or spoke about his approach, citing the difficulty in writing about something experiential and spontaneous as though it were a concrete, learnable technique. Moreover, he is sometimes criticized for lacking technique and relying on his charisma. When he cites spontaneity as an indicator of family health, one wonders if being charismatic is actually his technique in a nutshell.

Related ideas can be found in Yalom (the healing relationship); Satir (spontaneity as authenticity); Schneider (invoking the actual); Minuchin (read this book and forget about it).

Role Fluidity. Whitaker did not believe in fixed roles in families. He believed that sometimes a child could act as a mother, or a parent as a sibling, or a grandparent as a spouse. When he states (1981) that spontaneity is a key indicator of health, he means that a family locked into fixed roles has lost something essential to its health.

The ability to take on whatever role is needed at the time is also the ability to respond to changing circumstances. Psychopathology might be defined as developing a fixed set of responses to a given environment and then failing to change those responses when the environment changes; thus the family that can switch roles at need is one that can adapt healthily to a fluid world.

Related ideas can be found in Yalom (authenticity); Schneider (invoking the actual); Minuchin (diagrams, the rules, adaptability).

Self-disclosure. Whitaker espoused limited self-disclosure. He would not tell the family everything about himself for the sake of doing so, but he had no qualms about revealing relevant experiences, particularly in the rapport-building phases of therapy.

Related ideas can be found in Yalom (here and now orientation and limited disclosure).

Use of the self in therapy and doing one's own work. Being the change agent requires being comfortable with rejection. Whitaker was notorious for making bald and even rude comments in the service of unbalancing the family (Whitaker, 1978). A person who relies on others for approval and esteem is unlikely to be able to function well as a

Symbolic Experiential therapist, as this type of comment is likely to produce conflict and provoke hostility. Whitaker implied through this practice that, while therapeutic alliance and relationship are important, it is not necessary to be liked by one's families. As Dias (2010) writes: "a well-liked provocateur is no provocateur at all" (p. 1).

Another potential implication is one of trust. Generously, Whitaker often skirted the line between irreverence and disrespect. In doing so, he illustrated that he was not afraid of conflict, and that he was confident his relationships with his families could survive any temporary discomfort.

This type of intrinsic lesson is central to his theory of Symbolic Experiential therapy. He further asserts that the way one practices therapy is dependent on one's personal history and personality just as much as the present situation of a family is dependent on their collective and personal histories (Keith & Whitaker, 1991). Inasmuch as his patients are a part of his history, he learned to do therapy by doing it, and each new patient or family necessitates that learning over again.

Keith and Whitaker (1991) add that part of assessment is reading one's own responses. Anxiety is a key metric for the therapist; additionally, one reviews body state (tension, sexual arousal), access to primary process (perhaps best characterized by craziness or spontaneity), one's own body language and metacommunication and so on.

Keith and Whitaker (1991) also advocate joining the system: experience is intrinsic to change, and unbalancing the system from inside is the preferred method (see Symbolic Experiential Therapy, above). Joining is done by a process of mutual transference: the therapists develop empathy for the family, and pick up the language, tone, rhythm and postures of the family. Therapists must also play with the children.

Indeed, play is such an intrinsic part of this work that a therapist who favors dignity over fun ought to try a different approach (see "play and irreverence" below).

Napier and Whitaker (1978) also advocate developing one's own style; a slavish devotion to techniques keeps the therapist from being able to regress with the system and then grow with the system. Whitaker thinks the Experiential approach is difficult or impossible to teach owing to its idiosyncratic nature and reliance on the personality (and personhood) of the therapist as it does; he advocates, rather, observing the therapy in action, developing an eclectic style, and then maturing into a style of one's own.

Related ideas can be found in Yalom (we all face the same ultimate concerns, authenticity, the healing relationship, here and now orientation and limited disclosure); Schneider (awe, liberation, meaning); Frankl (meaning); May (encounter); Bowen (coaching, societal emotional process); Satir (connectedness and experiential learning); Minuchin (joining the system, experiential approach); Perls (look inside, look outside, now I am aware…).

Directiveness. Whitaker (1978) was frequently quite directive and active in therapy, in contrast to many other practitioners. This seems to have been in aid of destabilizing the family system; a family able to direct itself might most likely direct itself towards homeostasis. However, Whitaker did not speak or write directly about his high level of directiveness.

Craziness and Trickiness. Whitaker (1983) values adaptability and spontaneity. Rigid systems as well as rigid people are signs of dysfunction. Therefore he views madness as a sort of unfiltered responding, an unbridled creativity that is actually quite helpful. Similarly, trickiness represents a sort of supreme adaptability, a capacity to be unfazed by events.

Craziness as creativity is not necessarily negative, but not necessarily positive either. Keith and Whitaker (1991) allude to the functionality of the creativity: is the creativity of the individual engaged by the system, or is it devoted to a state of chaos? Is the creativity of the system engaged in a social context, or is the family isolated and eccentric?

In this context, pathology becomes a pragmatic matter. Three kinds of crazy emerge from this thinking: driven crazy, or removed from a system and thereby in a lost state of pseudo-chaos, existing in a new environment unconditioned to one's presence and looking for reactions to obsolete behaviors; going crazy, or embracing unconditional positive regard as a place of freedom of choice and expression, unbounded by systemic requirements; and acting crazy, or regressing into one of the previously described states in order to get one's needs met.

Related ideas can be found in Rollo May (The Daimonic); Minuchin (adaptability).

Play and irreverence. Keith and Whitaker (1991) suggests that play and irreverence are means of accessing absurdity. It is difficult to become too obsessed with the problems of living when one grasps the essential humor underlying our daily plights. A father growing rageful with his child might observe this behavior and then gently mock himself, acting out the role of enraged father in a fit of buffoonery. Irreverence for one's problems allows greater flexibility, and the ability to play magnifies irreverence.

Part of the therapist's role, then, is as a coach in learning the new skills of play, irreverence and absurdity. The therapist's own comments are playful and irreverent and point to the therapeutic value of recognizing the absurd. While structured activities are not part of Symbolic Experiential Therapy, organizing themes of playfulness is. Encouraging Father to argue with a son about the son dating Mother, for example, reframes present jealousy in an absurd way, making it more accessible and amenable to affective process.

Limited Encounter. Where other authors speak of authenticity and encounter, Whitaker (1983) was more interested in being whatever was necessary to keep the family unbalanced and in becoming the instrument of change. It was necessary for him to encounter the family, but he thought listening to them too much might be hypnotic and ineffective; joining the family on their terms would be counterproductive. Thus he used his great charisma to forge alliance quickly, and then became oppositional and directive, more interested in change than knowledge.

Related ideas can be found in Yalom (we all face the same ultimate concerns, authenticity, the healing relationship, here and now orientation and limited disclosure); Schneider (awe, liberation, meaning); Frankl (meaning); May (encounter); Bowen (coaching, societal emotional process); Satir (connectedness and experiential learning, the monad); Minuchin (joining the system, experiential approach); Perls (look inside, look outside, now I am aware…).

Diagnosis. Whitaker (1983) believes in limited encounter; that is, he wants to meet the family organism where it is, rather than encountering his own fantasies about the family or its members. He suggests that diagnoses are a way of pinning down the person, collecting a snapshot of them in a moment of time that probably better represents one's own nosology than the process of being that is the person. Like Yalom (above), Keith and Whitaker (1991) state that all pathology is interpersonal.

Diagnostics in this framework is largely irrelevant and thus informal. Whitaker searches for elements of the past that are maladaptive to the present, such as frozen myth systems, ghosts (absent family members still exerting an influence on those present), how the two families of origin are competing to have their systems replayed in this new system, triangulation and detriangulation, and so on. As to individual pathology, there can be no healthy members of a dysfunctional system; anyone in such a system that looks too well is probably devoted to the health of the system in some way (even via detachment: they need to grow up and learn to handle their own problems) which is inherently unhealthy, as a healthy system does not require such ministrations. Furthermore, were these efforts successful, the dedicated healer would be obsolete; therefore the efforts are ineffective and thus pathological (see "craziness and trickiness" above).

Given this framework, symptoms are reframed as the system's efforts towards growth. Affect is blocked at some point in the system and the system is attempting to adapt to an individual change that is covert; making that change overt (revealing the secret) by freeing up the blocked affect allows the system to adapt as needed. Symptoms and pathology then become obsolete; they may recrudesce at a future time when the events of the family life-cycle lead to another blockage but, if the family has learned adaptability, play and absurdity, the chances are reduced.

Related ideas can be found in Yalom (all problems are interpersonal problems); May (The Daimonic); Bowen (Nuclear Family Emotional System, Societal Emotional Process); Minuchin (family pathology); Laing (mental illness).

Family life cycle. The purpose of a marriage is for two families of origin to compete (battle) to perpetuate their respective ways of doing business through their children, who ultimately will spin off to perpetuate whichever family of origin won the battle (Whitaker, 1978, 1981). Whitaker here acknowledges that families have a life cycle and a purpose, however cynically he states that purpose.

Keith and Whitaker (1991) also describe the life cycle in technical Systemic terms, as the evolution of a system that changes while maintaining its integrity. The markers in such a change might be obvious (such as death, birth and marriages) or more subtle (father quits drinking, mother gets religion). As a rule, the developmental stages of the family's children define most of the family process; the differences in the needs of a couple vs. an infant, a family with an infant vs. a family with a toddler and so on are inescapable.

Moreover, stresses on a system tend to accumulate. Whitaker (1978) posits the most volatile time in a system is adolescence: the children are individuating while the parents are entering midlife with its attendant crises and the grandparents entering their elder years with those attendant crises. Here we have a system with three generations entering some type of personal crisis and looking to the system to help cope with the feelings these crises generate, as well as the system needing to accommodate behavioral changes from many individuals simultaneously.

These stresses are "serial impasses" that need to be accommodated or overcome. Affect lubricates this process; the feelings each person has become part and parcel of the system and the feelings of others help provide additional information to navigate individual crises. A new system emerges with the changed individual being more or less free to enter and leave the system as needed.

When affect is blocked, these impasses become real systemic crises; the system is unable to adapt to the changes because it lacks both data and motivation to do so. Positive affect, while desirable, is insufficient; all affect needs to flow freely through the system.

Related ideas can be found in Yalom (everyone faces the same ultimate concerns); Schneider (awe, invoking the actual); Frankl (meaning); Satir (freedom and responsibility); Minuchin (family life cycle).

Affect lubricates process. Things learned overtly and verbally are not so likely to stick as things learned covertly and non-verbally inasmuch as the memory system is tied to the limbic system. Processes that take place in the context of an emotional discharge will be more effective at promoting change than those taking place in a flat, disconnected fashion. Thus Whitaker urges therapists to not be afraid of affect, any affect, from the clients.

Myths. Every family has myths that are more or less accurate. For Keith and Whitaker (1991), the accuracy of a myth is less important than that the family be able to tolerate changes to the myth. That is, a mythology that does not evolve with the system becomes burdensome; the family becomes disconnected from its history. These myths define roles and, as seen above, roles that are too static lock a system into dysfunction. If roles are flexible (which first necessitates that myths are flexible), then the family is better able to meet its emotional needs fluidly.

Related ideas can be found in Yalom (interpretation); Related ideas can be found in Schneider (the truth); May (myth); Minuchin (diagrams, family myth and narrative).

Trianglulation. Napier and Whitaker accept the idea of triangulation as described by Bowen (1978). They give a dramatic description of the process:

> Look at it this way: David and Carolyn developed a mutually agreed-upon distance in their marriage. For the moment, never mind *why* – it just happened. David didn't do it; Carolyn didn't do it. The both did it – by gradual degrees, over a period of years, and unconsciously. But the psychological space between the couple didn't remain a vacuum. Into it moved their children, most prominently Claudia. Nor were the spouses merely cool and aloof from each other. As Claudia grew, she became a pawn in the unspoken but intense conflict between her parents. David could meet some of his needs for emotional closeness by snuggling up to his daughter, and Carolyn could express some of her anger at David indirectly – by yelling at Claudia instead of David. The couple lived vicariously, indirectly, through their daughter. And this situation was obviously very confusing and painful for Claudia. (p.84, italics in orginal)

Related ideas can be found in Yalom (authenticity, the healing relationship); Schneider (invoking the actual, vivifying and confronting resistances and self protections); May (courage, encounter); Satir (congruence, the monad, self-esteem vs. shame, connectedness and experiential learning); Minuchin (diagrams, rules); Laing (mental illness); Perls (encounter).

Givens of Family Existence. Kaye, Dichter and Keith (1986) note the worldview associated with Symbolic Experiential Family Therapy. The first is that life is confusing, complex, paradoxical and painful; for example, one's capacity to be intimate with another person depends on one's capacity to first individuate, just as courage requires fear and faith requires doubt. Pain is just a part of the process and is eminently bearable. What is unbearable is one's belief that pain can (or should) be cured.

Next is the ultimate freedom of the human to choose its own course. Initiative is sacred (p. 522). Growth that results from coercion (compliance or defiance) is not really growth.

Third, crisis tends to initiate change. People change when the pain of changing is less than the pain of not changing. Thus a crisis might push one into acting differently and experiencing the potentially positive feedback from that action.

Fourth, these givens are givens-that is, unchangeable. The facts of the matter do not change, but how the family perceives and responds to these facts can. This approach emphasizes the limits of being, particularly the presence of emotions and our responsibility for those emotions, over the idea of potential. As a corollary, Kaye et al. (1986) suggest that emotion is a type of experience that can be reacted to just as any other. Thus it is not anger about a situation that cripples us, but shame or fear or anger about that anger.

Fifth and final is the idea of failure as teacher. Failure is inevitable (following the theme of limitation). Success is needed as well as failure but unless one can experience failure and experience surviving failure and learning from it, one must remain afraid (phobic) of failure forever.

Related ideas can be found in Yalom (we all face the same ultimate concerns); Schneider (liberation, vivifying and confronting resistances and self-protections, paradox, meaning, constriction vs. expansion); Frankl (meaning, freedom); May (courage, angst, anxiety, will); Whitaker (family life cycle, givens of family existence, myth); Minuchin (family life cycle, family myth and narrative).

Salvadore Minuchin

Minuchin is an Ecuadorian therapist responsible for creating Structural Family Therapy. He is aware of and takes an interest in Existentialism (e.g. 1984, pp 195, 196) but makes no statements regarding a position on Existential thought per se.

Joining the system. Minuchin (1974) believes in joining the system in order to provide positive feedback; this feedback helps disrupt dysfunctional relationship patterns and stabilizes around new patterns or behaviors. More specifically, he enters the various subsystems within a family system and intervenes with them in ways that require adaptation. This requires keeping multiple views in mind: the identified patient's with their own behavior and personality as well as each subsystem and the whole system in the context of society. He writes of this experience:

Looking into the interior of a family, one can suddenly be caught by scenarios. These may be whimsical, challenging, absurd or dramatic, but they are all disturbing because they carry the tantalizing feeling that they are complete. It is as if one glanced into a store window, and flashed the universe.

But the truth is that the family therapist is always in the presence of shifting images. Often he focuses on one well-defined piece – the family's presentation of their identified patient. But there are hundreds of other pieces with clear or uneven edges that have to be fitted together in order to see the pattern, and

perhaps change the position of the pieces. (Minuchin, 1984, p. 7)

He presumes the changes that occur in the subsystem to be stable over time due to

his insertion of positive feedback and the greater functionality afforded by new

interactional methods. Moreover (1974), a subsystem operates best when encased in

strong boundaries (i.e., lacking interference from third parties, especially

intergenerationally). Part of the intervention is the redrawing of the boundaries, which

may be done explicitly (verbally) or merely by interacting with people as though they

were a subsystem. A subsystem absent of triangulations is more effective, and more

effective transactions tend to perpetuate.

Once one subsystem has made a change, Minuchin moves onto the next; this

process of moving from subsystem to subsystem is called sequential processing. A joint

process would include all family members together (Barth, 1990).

To join the system (or subsystem) effectively, one must first accommodate to

them. This means picking up and using their language, recognizing their needs,

mirroring, offering positive support, and keeping one's wits in terms of observing process

and content. In Minuchin's own words (1974):

> As a therapist, I tend to act like a distant relative. I like to tell anecdotes about my
>
> own experiences and thinking, and to include things I have read or heard that are
>
> relevant to the particular family. I try to assimilate the family's language and to
>
> build metaphors using the family's language and myths. These methods telescope
>
> time, investing an encounter between strangers with the affect of an encounter

between old acquaintances. They are accommodation techniques, which are vital to the process of joining. (p. 122)

An implication of this joining and accommodation is the idea that the therapist must feel the joy and pain of being part of the system; they ought to feel the rejection of being left out of a conversation, the validation of being heard, and so on. They ought to follow these feelings towards the transactions at which they point and leverage the feelings into data and intervention.

Joining may include or imply maintenance, which means active support for the rules of a particular subsystem (Minuchin, 1974). This might be done when something is working well as it is, or if it is too early in the process to intervene with the particular subsystem at the time. Additionally, one might paradoxically maintain a transaction in order to highlight its ineffectiveness (such as prescribing the behavior).

Related ideas can be found in Yalom (we all face the same ultimate concerns, authenticity, the healing relationship, here and now orientation and limited disclosure); Schneider (awe, liberation, meaning); Frankl (meaning); May (encounter); Bowen (coaching, societal emotional process); Satir (connectedness and experiential learning, the monad); Whitaker (limited encounter, use of self in therapy and doing one's own work); Perls (look inside, look outside, now I am aware...).

Family pathology. Minuchin states that no individual is sick; rather, their relationships (or system) are sick. Thus the treatment for any given psychopathology lies within the relationships the person has rather than their genes or cognitions. Treatment means disrupting those relationships, providing positive feedback, and helping the members of the system cohere around a new relationship (Minuchin, 1974).

Related ideas can be found in Yalom (all problems are interpersonal problems); May (The Daimonic); Bowen (Nuclear Family Emotional System, Societal Emotional Process); Whitaker (diagnosis); Laing (mental illness).

Diagrams. Minuchin diagrams relationships within a system in order to illustrate dysfunction (or, theoretically, function). Thus, at least a minimal level of understanding or insight is required from the family; change is fostered through insight and agency (Minuchin, 1974.)

The diagrams (which he calls "maps") typically include boundaries and power. Power in a system should be consolidated with the parents; a diagram showing a parent in a sibling relationship with the children or with the children above (in power over) the parents indicates a serious systemic dysfunction, regardless of its relative necessity.

He refers to these maps as lacking the richness of the actual ecology the way a map of a territory lacks the richness of the land itself; it is a stop-motion snapshot of a system that is changing and evolving. Its utility lies in the map's ability to help the therapist make sense of all the data they are collecting in that moment, but will require constant revision in the light of new data and results from interventions.

Minuchin mentions Transactions (1974) without elucidating the whole theory of Transactional Analysis. He states quite simply that every interaction between one family member and another is a sort of transaction and stands a certain chance of becoming habitual (homeostatic). Identifying patterns of transactions helps create the maps needed to choose points of intervention.

Related ideas can be found in Yalom (interpretation).

The rules. Part of the analysis of a family is understanding its rules. Each family will have its own unique rules, but the rules will tend to cohere around certain predictable concepts. For example, one rule might be who makes the rules, or how they are agreed upon. This might take a functional or a dysfunctional form and might be more or less covert but is usually present in some fashion. Who is allowed to side with whom is similarly thematic; perhaps the father, in order to preserve harmony with the mother, must usually take her side against the children. Boundaries are another sort of rule and impact individuation.

The rules are often codified into the relational patterns noted in the diagrams Minuchin uses to foster insight (Minuchin, 1974.)

The rules also include the nature of the family's boundaries. The boundaries are the rules of engagement around how family members (or subsystems) can communicate with one another. Minuchin advocates for moderately flexible boundaries that change with varying stressors. Boundaries range from enmeshment at the most flexible (see Bowen's "differentiation," above) to rigidity (see Bowen's "emotional disengagement" above). Most families fall in the center of this continuum and are healthy. An extreme position at either end of the polarity would be pathological.

The rules can and should change over the long term (lifecycle) and also the short term (external stressors). When the rules are too rigid, the system cannot adapt to changing circumstances and becomes pathological.

Related ideas can be found in Yalom (authenticity); Schneider (vivifying and confronting resistance); May (encounter); Bowen (triangulation); Satir (shame vs. self-esteem); Whitaker (role fluidity); Perls (encounter).

Adaptability. The rules tend to appear on a spectrum between flexibility and rigidity. Too much flexibility can appear as chaos or anarchy; too much rigidity can appear as authoritarianism. In either case, the family's ability to react coherently to changing circumstances and changing needs is impaired.

For Minuchin, the healthy family is one that walks the middle path between rigidity and flexibility, having appropriate, semi-permeable boundaries and roles (Minuchin, 1974.)

Related ideas can be found in Yalom (authenticity); Schneider (vivifying and confronting resistance); May (encounter); Bowen (differentiation, triangulation); Satir (shame vs. self-esteem); Whitaker (role fluidity); Perls (encounter).

Experiential approach. While insight seems to be an inherent part of the process, Minuchin uses many experiential methods to achieve change. He cuts subsystems out from the herd, for example, by changing seating arrangements. He behaves as part of a subsystem, forcing it to adapt to his presence, and always works to produce unbalancing events (Minuchin, 1974).

Another way of referring to the experiential approach is "enactment." This means vivifying the dysfunction by seeing it played out in the therapy room, seeing the dysfunctional process rather than hearing complaints. When the dysfunctions are readily available, the therapist points them out, making plain the missed communications and unsuccessful interactions (Barth, 1990).

Related ideas can be found in Yalom (we all face the same ultimate concerns, authenticity, the healing relationship, here and now orientation and limited disclosure); Schneider (awe, liberation, meaning); Frankl (meaning); May (encounter); Bowen (coaching, societal emotional process); Satir (connectedness and experiential learning, the monad); Whitaker (limited encounter, use of self in therapy and doing one's own work); Perls (look inside, look outside, now I am aware...).

Family Life Cycle. Families go through predictable stages of development: the making of the couple; accommodating to young children; people entering and leaving the system via death, divorce, birth and remarriage; raising adolescent children; adult children leaving or extending the system (Minuchin & Fishman, 1981).

These stages are ultimately unavoidable as time marches ever forward. Dysfunction in family systems can involve getting hung up or stuck at the transition point between these life-cycle phases (for example, the children rejecting their mother's new spouse or the parents of a disabled adult relating to them as though they were at a previous level of development).

A system that is unduly rigid or inflexible cannot adapt to such changes and attempts to relate in the same way as ever despite obviously different circumstances and needs. A system that is too flexible makes no effort to adapt to changing circumstances; the system is in perpetual chaos and the addition or subtraction of elements is scarcely relevant. A system with inadequate coping may become more rigid when entering periods of stress such as major system milestones (births, deaths, etc.), and become unable to recognize the utility of temporary changes in structure.

Related ideas can be found in Yalom (we all face the same ultimate concerns); Frankl (meaning); Schneider (awe, meaning, vivifying and confronting resistances and self protections, invoking the actual); May (courage, angst, anxiety, myth); Bowen (differentiation, triangulation); Satir (Chaos); Whitaker (family life cycle).

Read this book and then forget about it. Minuchin and Fishman (1981) states that spontaneity is key to addressing systemic problems. The use of techniques, they contend, is tantamount to manipulation for power (p. 1). Thus a person is qualified to call them self a therapist only after technique has been mastered and transcended into an art, much like a technically proficient iceskater must first learn to jump and then forget all the technical aspects of jumping in order to jump artfully.

Related ideas can be found in Yalom (authenticity, the healing relationship, here and now orientation and limited disclosure); Schneider (invoking the actual, vivifying and confront resistances and self-protections); May (courage, The Daimonic); Bowen (triangles); Whitaker (use of self in therapy and doing your own work, personal involvement); Minuchin (read this book and forget about it); Laing (mental illness).

Myths and narratives. The rules can be created (and enforced or maintained) by belief in family myths and narratives (Minuchin, 1999). These myths and narratives are stories the family tells itself about its origins, values, and purpose. The power of myth and narrative to keep a system homeostatic is substantial.

One way to intervene to change the rules in a positive direction is to help the family tell itself a new story or reinterpret the old story such that a dysfunctional myth is replaced with something more positive or functional. A family might believe, for example, in some sort of family burden or curse; all sorts of evidence might exist for an almost inevitable suffering or loss (take, for example, the Kennedy family). The therapist, seeing that this family myth leads towards some negative attitude and behavior (such as over-valuing sons over daughters), the therapist can help the family reinterpret the meaning of previous losses or challenges (for example, to find the value in grief if the evidence of extraordinary loss is present or to value the family life-cycle more clearly if the evidence is exaggerated).

Related ideas can be found in Yalom (interpretation); Frankl (meaning); May (meaning, myth).

R. D. Laing

Laing was a Scottish psychiatrist whose works covered a great deal of territory, including (separately) a strong Existential influence and some work on Systemic thought (e.g., 1964). He wrote extensively on the subject of psychosis, alluding to family or social rather than simple psychological causes for madness.

Mental Illness. Laing (1960, 1961, 1964) did not deny the existence of mental illness, but he did challenge the diathesis-stress model and denied the medical basis of psychosis. He was more interested in the social, Systemic and psychological phenomena associated with madness.

He posited that families created double-binds on their children by introducing contradictory, mutually incompatible demands; rather than make these demands the fault of the parents, he made them the fault of the larger system in which the parents existed (namely society). These double-binds in the system that produced the self of the child led to so-called insanity which, for Laing, was in fact a reasonable person's adjustment to unreasonable personality demands.

Furthermore, he viewed psychosis not as something incomprehensible to the non-psychotic, but as an attempt by the person to communicate their emotional state while still meeting the divided demands placed upon them by their family of origin and their current circumstances or broader system.

Laing (1967) also characterized psychosis as a rational defense against impossible odds. He thought it might be sick to be pronounced sane in a sick society, that the psychotic who has split off from society and engagement does so because the alternative – to remain engaged with a sick society in which, perhaps, the worst has already happened– is worse. Perhaps the best defense for a war hero who remembers all the lives he has taken is madness, and perhaps it is equally mad to ask him to return to sanity (and its attendant contradictory demands such as pride and shame).

Laing's influence is questionable overall, but this means of relating to people in severe states can still be found in Existential thought (e.g., Mendelowitz, 2008) and relates to the Systemic thought that there is no mental illness, only systemic problems with relationships (e.g., Minuchin, 1974).

Related ideas can be found in Yalom (we all face the same ultimate concerns, all problems are interpersonal problems); Bowen (differentiation, triangulation, nuclear family emotional process); Minuchin (family pathology).

Interexperience. Laing (1967) disapproved of the behavioristic trends of his time. He asserted that the science of psychology could not lie in the mere observation of behavior, as behavior tells nothing of the experience of the person being observed.

He acknowledged that it is impossible to experience the experiences of another and yet he thought it was vital to try, referring to therapy as "an obstinate attempt of two persons to recover the wholeness of being human through the relationship between them" (1967, p.63).

He called his science of trying to comprehend the experience of another person "interexperience" (p. 17). One attempts to understand the other not only by observing their behavior but also by observing one's experience of the behavior of the other. Then one behaves in response to this experience, and observes and experiences behavior in return.

Thus the other person is experienced, and some of their experience can be gleaned subjectively and in a limited fashion.

Fritz Perls

Perls advocated what he called Gestalt Therapy. This is the idea that everything exists in a certain context, with attention shifting between foreground and background objects within the scope of perception. Additionally, it presupposes that people are, ultimately, indivisible into smaller parts (such as ego, superego and id). His mode of Gestalt therapy focuses largely on helping people incorporate all their disowned thoughts and feelings.

Look inside, look outside. Perls (1969/1992) invited people to first examine their feelings, thoughts, body states and comment on them, and then to refer to the therapist in some manner. This shifting from internal to external referent was intended to help people become more grounded in their context as well as more internally integrated.

Related ideas can be found in Yalom (we all face the same ultimate concerns, authenticity, the healing relationship, here and now orientation and limited disclosure); Schneider (awe, liberation, meaning); Frankl (meaning); May (encounter); Bowen (coaching, societal emotional process); Satir (connectedness and experiential learning); Whitaker (use of self in therapy and doing one's own work, directiveness); Minuchin (joining the system, experiential approach).

Now I am aware. Perls (1969/1992, 1981) invited people to describe their experiences in the present tense, as though happening now. Most commonly, this was in the instruction to begin each sentence with the words, "Now I am aware…" and then describe some internal event (be it a memory, a feeling, a thought, or an emotion) as something literally in the present. Memories could be a special case, however, and he would ask that memories be described as though the events being examined were happening in the here and now, not as though the person were reliving the events but living them for the first time.

Perls' assumption was that the past is imaginary. Therefore, the only relevant way to work with the past is in the present, with the people with whom we are present.

The Importance of Subjective Data. Perls (1973) notes that subjective data is vital to understand a person. Their experiences and perceptions, regardless of the intersections between those phenomena and objective, external reality, really are the person being understood. Insight, therefore, must come from some understanding of these subjective processes rather than understanding of objective reality. The person seeing reality, then, is at least as important as reality.

It is not even very important that the therapist understand the patient's subjective experience so much as it is important for the person to live, communicate and own that experience. The therapist is helpful inasmuch as they provide an external referent to the subjective.

Encounter. Perls (1973) worked extensively with groups and couples. His idea of encounter is that each person would learn to become a referent for the other, an external marker for some internal experience, in a way that is mutually beneficial and honest. This honesty often crosses the border of short-term benefit, inasmuch as conflict has to be engaged when it is present; thus harmony in this moment is sacrificed to self-honesty and authenticity in the long run. The goal of couples' therapy, for example is not necessarily to improve or save a marriage, but to help people become more self-honest and thus honest with one another. Marriages might have to end for the relationships to move forward productively.

Related ideas can be found in Yalom (we all face the same ultimate concerns, authenticity, the healing relationship, here and now orientation and limited disclosure); Schneider (awe, liberation, meaning); Frankl (meaning); May (encounter, courage); Bowen (coaching, societal emotional process); Satir (connectedness and experiential learning); Whitaker (limited encounter, symbolic experiential treatment); Minuchin (joining the system, experiential approach).

Summary

This chapter has provided an overview of the pertinent literature from Existential theorists (Yalom, May, Schneider and Frankl), from Systemic theorists (Bowen, Satir, Whitaker, and Minuchin) and other pertinent writers (Laing, Perls). Their ideas have been parsed for what seems most germane to this discussion and then presented in a format of headings, discussion, and cross-references to similar ideas from other theorists.

Methodology

This chapter outlines the process of developing this dissertation from inception to completion, including the research biases of the author, inspiration for conducting this research, the process of settling on this research method, and the limitations of the findings.

Inspiration

The author began practicing with families and Systemic treatment design during practicum and was gratified by being able to be of service during this experience. Later, he became interested in Existential Psychotherapy and found the thinking and methods of that practice more satisfactory than some of those native to Family Systems therapy. Retaining an interest in both fields but not wanting to practice very differently in two contexts, he decided to find out if there was a rational basis for practicing with families in an Existential context. Support for this idea came from a number of fronts, including personal communication with Albert Chan who practices Family Therapy in Hong Kong and does so with an Existential basis in mind.

Deciding on the method

Initially, the author considered other kinds of research. These included a quantitative study on the effectiveness of Existential methods in Family therapy and a qualitative study into the Existential experiences of family in therapy, meaning what sort of experiences were had that entered into boundary territory (see Yalom, below). These studies were discussed at length with university staff and classmates but were difficult to write about. The difficulty seemed to stem from lacking a strong theoretical basis from which to proceed. With no theory from which to distill an hypothesis, formulating an experiment (either qualitative or quantitative) was very difficult.

Along the way, the author heard about a third type of paper: the theoretical dissertation. More than a treatment manual, this methodology appealed to the author's preference for philosophic discourse and seemed to be the missing piece in common with his other beginning inquiries into the subject. This dissertation represents the culmination of a long preparation in the study of Existentialism and Systemic thinking. It has changed form and format many times and has evolved even during its writing towards a sleeker, more targeted inquiry. It has become a sort of qualitative meta-analysis rather than a pure philosophic or theoretical discourse, and this seems to serve the need as stated currently.

This comparative study compares and contrasts writings from the seemingly disparate fields of Existential and Systemic therapy with the intent of integrating these fields into a coherent whole. The integration of therapy modalities means a sensible examination of two or more modes of therapy resulting in a cogent theory that relies on both bodies of knowledge. If the integration is successful, we expect to see synthesis–that is, the resulting body of knowledge is greater than and produces superior results to either body of knowledge prior to integration.

Process

The first stage of this project has been an immersion in the literature, including the philosophic material from Existentialism and Systemic thinking as well as the theoretical literature from Existential Psychotherapy and Family Systems Therapy. This process has required some degree of selectivity; there are more authors on these subjects than it is reasonable to read or to review, and each author reviewed has written more material than can be comprehensively represented in any form shorter than the original works. Moreover, in quantitative research, error variance can be introduced into studies by comparing multiple data sets. That is, the more sets of data compared to other sets of data, the more likely it is that spurious correlations will be found through error (randomness). The same is likely to be possible with this sort of qualitative analysis: the more material is reviewed, the more material will appear similar to other material, and the more difficult it will be to state that the similarities point us towards underlying themes rather than random coincidences. Finally, along the way there has been some question as to how to select and reject authors and which material to include from each, with some understandable push for more comprehensiveness and diversity of thought.

This dilemma – between increasing comprehensiveness and keeping the field of material manageable – is not easily resolved. The author looked to the field of quantitative study for guidance. While researchers make some claim to objectivity, the process of selecting data to compare always involves subjective judgment, namely an hypothesis (or null hypothesis). The quantitative researcher does not select phenomena they do not believe will be related; as noted above, comparing everything to everything increases error variance and is therefore bad science.

Thus the authors specifically studied have been limited to: Yalom, Schneider, Frankl and May from the Existentialists; Bowen, Satir, Whitaker and Minuchin from the Systemic thinkers; and Laing and Perls, whose work covers aspects of Existential and Systemic thought. These thinkers were selected because the author of this paper thinks it likely that their contributions to their relative fields are likely to show some correlation.

In addition, they are widely held to be founders of their respective ways of thinking and therefore not unduly derivative or repetitive, which would be another potential source of spurious correlation.

It is for this reason that many writers have been excluded that do seem to bear on the problem at hand. In the course of this study, the author read a great many books and book chapters which are not included in the review of literature for the practical reason that they do not bear directly on the problem at hand. However, all of the readings and additionally attendance at conferences, discussions with luminaries in the field, practical experience and supervision, all have some bearing in the interpretation of the material that is included and the distillation of some form of philosophy. For example, Van Kaam (1966) provides an excellent integration of Existential thought up to his time, including very meaningful work on the ethics of will in psychotherapy, but is derivative (p. 15). Indeed, it is his phenomenology which inspires this work. Similarly Bugental and a host of Systemic writers and thinkers, while brilliant, have been excluded due to derivation, repetition, or lack of impact on the field at large.

The second stage has been an attempt to deduce the validity of the ideas encountered during this immersion. Given little objective guidance, the author has used his own sense of resonance with the material, his own instincts as to what is relevant and true. To borrow from Van Kaam: "To secure at least an initial and relative intersubjective agreement, I conducted this phenomenological research in dialogue with the descriptions given by some of the scholars who attempted the same…" (p. 15).

Another roadmap to integration is Duhl & Duhl (1991). Their Intergrative Family Therapy is a way of trying to keep track of advances in Systemic theory in a rational manner. They consider their work a gazetteer (p.486) of approaches, an atlas full of roadmaps applicable in different places, a toolbox full of useful things to pull out in therapy as needed and fitting, as well as just one snapshot of an evolving theory.

At one level, their integration is really eclecticism: the component theories and interventions are not combined to form a synthesis, only used when deemed appropriate. At another level, there is some degree of integration: there is one underlying theory of systemic work (including respect for pain, respect for parents, spontaneity as genuineness, the usefulness of defenses, belief in individuals in systems rather than an anthropomorphic system with its own needs and experience, a relativistic view of reality, therapists as humans and change agents, and respect for the will of the patient or family, otherwise called non-directiveness). Within this underlying theory, Duhl and Duhl posit that the therapist must be aware of their own Gestalt – that is, everything is happening in a particular context, and reality is determined by where the therapist chooses to focus, background or foreground, which object in which field.

This is all to say that Duhl and Duhl recognize the danger of reifying any one theory; all theories are equally true and equally false, mere metaphors to help the therapist frame and comprehend their observations and experiences. Into this multiplicity of fields come the diverging theories of Family Systems, each useful at particular times.

The work of the following chapters will be to make sense of the literature reviewed earlier in the study. A beginning has been made on this work with a sort of preliminary concept-mapping or tagging; each idea from each theorist has been connected to other ideas from other theorists using the format, "Related ideas can be found in …" This will serve as a way of preorganizing the material for its synthesis in the next chapter.

Chapter IV will lean heavily on this preorganization as a roadmap for synthesis. The next section, Findings, will explore the relationships noted between ideas and begin to formulate a synthesis of these ideas.

As noted in the beginning pages of this project, the methods used here are neither quantitative nor strictly qualitative but rather a philosophical, theoretical inquiry. As such, there exist standard limitations to the inquiry, inasmuch as the data generated will conform to neither mode of discovery noted. There will be no objective data sets; in fact, as the author will use previously published work, studies and expert opinions in the field, no data will be generated at all. There will be no null hypotheses, nothing proven nor disproven. Rather, the outcome will be a theoretical framework upon which one can hang the sorts of questions that can produce these sorts of answers.

Like Duhl and Duhl (1991), this document attempts to provide roadmaps of current and past techniques, philosophy and theory. Unlike Duhl and Duhl, it also attempts to get to synthesis: rational integration will result in two theories reducing to one theory that explains more with fewer terms. Rather than taking a block of clay and adding more and more clay until the desired shape emerges, integration takes a block of wood and whittles down everything extraneous until the needed shape emerges; moreover, the whittler saw that shape in the wood from the beginning.

Findings

This chapter will examine the connections between the themes noted above, beginning with an assessment of ability to proceed and then examining specific points of confluence between each idea. This will be done cumulatively, such that ideas already mentioned as being confluent with previous ideas will not be mentioned again individually. Thus Congruence, which is discussed as being confluent with Authenticity, does not appear as its own heading in this review.

Ability to Proceed

Substantial confluence has been found between the theories reviewed (see figure 1). Within the fields of Existentialism and Systemic thought, there are more points of confluence than between the fields, suggesting perhaps that an adequate theory has been described on each side. Enough confluence seems to exist between the fields to proceed with the investigation, hopefully producing a third theory.

Ultimate Concerns	Paradox
Authenticity/congruence	Presence
Encounter	Expansion/contraction
Myth	Happiness
Experiential Focus	Centrality of being
Use of self in therapy	Family projection process
Reverence vs. Irreverence	Chaos vs. Homeostasis
Awe	Societal Emotional Process

Liberation	Spirituality
Rules	Pathology

Specific Confluences

Ultimate Concerns. A sort of universality of the struggles of being can be found in the writings of every author. Yalom (1980) writes of the finality and inescapability of death, as well as the universal struggles we have with freedom and responsibility, with meaninglessness (or thrownness and banality) and with our ultimate isolation. Schneider gives us the ideas of awe and presence, the universal needs to encounter and be encountered. Frankl (2006) identifies a component of meaning as being the way one faces inevitable, inescapable suffering. How one cleaves to one's values and expresses one's ultimate freedom when facing death, pain and deprivation are, for Frankl, the ultimate markers (and makers) of one's central being. May (1967) notes the will is inescapable and sometimes terrifying. He also cites that the things we deny in ourselves can come back to haunt us, giving us the Daimonic, another universal truth: our dark sides and our wills can be denied consciously but will be expressed regardless of our intent. Bowen (1978) writes along similar lines: individuals in families can address their anxieties with one another directly or suffer those anxieties indefinitely (disengagement). Furthermore, those unaddressed anxieties can be transmitted through generations and lived out by our children and our children's children, a sort of intergenerational Daimonic. Satir (1988) notes that we are all connected, regardless of our desires in this matter. Furthermore, her take on freedom seems to integrate an inescapable responsibility. And she notes that children must balance self esteem and shame according to the actions of their parents–something both inescapable and unchangeable. This brings in the idea of intentionality (also advocated by May)–that parents can intentionally teach their children self-esteem or unintentionally teach them shame. Whitaker notes certain unavoidable truths about the family life-cycle and the stresses of transition times in that cycle. Minuchin similarly notes the presence of stressors related to stages in family life and the necessity for the systems to change according to their component inhabitants. Families with teenaged children, for example, must function differently from those with infants, and their concerns must be different. Laing (1964) notes that the drive to live in accordance with the demands placed upon a person is universal; the need to express one's feelings regarding those demands is also universal. Psychosis, he contends, is a normal and healthy reaction to abnormal, unhealthy demands from families and society at large. Perls gives us the notion that people exist in an inescapable present context, and that we all choose what to attend to in a given environment. That we have feelings and needs is also inescapable. Finally, he seems to suggest that the struggle between long-term and short-term harmony is universal.

That there are Ultimate Concerns for families and that these concerns are a part of Systemic theory seems clear, as does the fact that they are related to (but not dependant on) the Ultimate Concerns of individuals.

Exactly how freedom or responsibility plays out systemically, for example, is complex. The research seems to indicate a need for differentiation, both from the individuals in the systems and the therapist/s. Will and intentionality play into one's decisions to either submit to unconscious manipulation through the emotions of other family members or to make active decisions based on that input. Systemic change can become a battle between conscious and unconscious elements – a conscious therapist manipulating an unconscious system, or a person making active decisions experiencing systemic chaos that threatens to drag him or her back away from change.

Information and insight contribute to the expression of will and intentionality as people can only choose behavior of which they are conscious. What constitutes insight might be a question for another day, but affective and empathic data as well as structural data seem to be present in the literature reviewed thus far.

Isolation is also relevant and also complex. One's decision to differentiate versus remaining enmeshed, for example, seems like a choice to embrace versus deny isolation (although the isolation is ultimately still present). The choice to cut off rather than engage the anxiety in a system is a more literal form of isolating. A more salient way of stating the problem might be to refer to engagement versus disengagement: to stay with the system and its problems or to divorce them and take one's share of the property (coping) away from the system.

Meaning seems present and related in the form of myths (or history) as well as the meaningfulness of engagement, that is, a lived life over one avoided rather than a post-hoc meaning or story told to unify the past into a cogent whole, or a meaning-in-the-moment. This sort of living without asking is related to the concept of awe.

Finally, death and limitation are clearly present in the family life-cycle, in role-fluidity versus rigidity. That the family encounters these problems is irrelevant; how they encounter them or fail to encounter them forms the basis for working with systems.

Schneider has a unique take on the ultimate concerns of existence with the use of Awe as both a perspective and a goal and the idea of expansion vs. contraction. These ideas are related to the Givens of Existence, but also foundational philosophical stances that need to be handled separately.

Authenticity/congruence. Every author reviewed had some corollary idea to authenticity or congruence. Yalom described authenticity in great detail. Schneider referred to presence and naivete, the willingness to be with the other, as well as the potential to expand or retreat in the face of living. He also noted that a consequence of being invoked to the actual and of living one's self-protections might be awe. Frankl noted the struggle to stay true to one's values, down to the final act of freedom: to try to be a good person in the face of inescapable suffering. May discussed the interlocking dimensions of courage, will, and intentionality. Bowen discussed differentiation and the benefits of openness and confrontation. Satir discussed congruence, the art of believing, thinking in accordance with that belief, talking about the thought, and acting in accordance with what one has said, as well as speaking and acting respectfully of one's intentions, of context, of environment and of the other. Whitaker wrote of being a change agent, of being the sort of person who does not contaminate their relationships with their own problems, of being able to play and encounter absurdity. Minuchin gives us the idea of technique as manipulation and of spontaneity as authentic, helpful engagement; of not trying to do something to or for the patient but being available to the relationship, part of the relationship. Laing notes that people with psychosis are trying to be authentic to conflicting, irreconcilable introjects – the idea, perhaps, that authenticity is not some abstract, post-hoc goal dreamed up by philosophers but actually a deep-seated human need. Perls gives us self-honesty, interpersonal honesty, and the need to look into our selves and feelings and then refer to the environment and our relationships as context for the inner state.

Authenticity in systems appears to be a conflict or tension between short-term harmony and long-term interpersonal honesty. A family is most functional when all of its members are functional; a family is least functional when one or more members are sacrificed to the coping needs of other members. When coping needs are put off onto subsystems or individuals, individual members are allowed to suppress or deny needs, feelings and conflicts, at a cost to other individuals in the system. This sort of disengagement with reality represents a kind of inauthenticity, a self-deception and other-deception that is damaging to long-term harmony.

Seen in this manner, short-term harmony (or failing to argue when argument is called for, repressing conflict or difficult affect for the sake of getting along in the moment) can be seen as inauthentic. This judgment might carry serious diversity problems, however, as short-term harmony might be more important to certain cultures than long-term interpersonal honesty. In this case, the sacrifice might carry important meaning and might not yield suffering as predicted by this model.

The movement towards long-term harmony, then, probably includes some means of maintaining short-term harmony while allowing for freedom of expression. More will be said of this in the last section.

Encounter. Each theorist notes the importance of interpersonal encounter in some context. Yalom writes extensively on the subject of authentic engagement both in individual and group psychotherapy. As noted above, he goes so far as to suggest that the therapeutic relationship might be all that matters, and everything we do as a therapist is really just context for that relationship. All problems are interpersonal problems and must be handled interpersonally, he suggests. The way one person affects another is important data in choicefulness and adaptation and often the most effective route to insight. Schneider invites his clients to presence by being present to them. This awe-filled presence forms the bedrock of a metaphoric roadway leading towards liberation. If the EI therapist is neither awe-filled nor presenceful, nothing of significance can happen in therapy. Frankl writes little about this form of engagement but does note that encounter with the other is a form of meaning. A life empty of encounter would be a life empty of meaning for Frankl, and meaning forms the basis for all of his work. May makes careful notes about the interrelatedness of love, care, will, and responsibility. One's ability to encounter another person despite the inevitability of loss and pain forms the basis for and reinforces courage, and courageous acts of encounter lead towards the meaning Frankl advocates. Bowen suggests that avoiding encounter is dangerous, leading to dysfunctional coping and pathology, disengagement and anxiety. Satir gives us interconnectedness and the powerfulness of congruent engagement. Moreover, she gives us her unswerving faith in humanity, and the healing power of engaging people and families from the basis of that unconditional positive regard. She writes about the importance of being a person who is of service to others, about first doing one's own work in order to be able to encounter families in a way that is wholesome and helpful. Whitaker similarly notes the importance of engaging authentically with people in families and helping the system learn through the experience of relationships and relatedness rather than the explication of themes and stories. Minuchin writes about joining and accommodation in order to help the therapist become part of – engage with – the system at hand. His ideas of positive feedback and destabilizing systems from the inside relate powerfully to the other ideas mentioned above. Laing suggests the possibility of engagement with psychotic patients and psychosis as communication. Perls writes explicitly about encounter and the needfulness of having a relationship to use as external referent in doing personal work. The implications of his ideas of encounter are not yet fully elucidated.

Here we have a strongly related set of ideas about encounter and interpersonal work in the context of a healing relationship. The task in a family system seems to be to teach the family to relate to one another in ways that are helpful, genuine, and intentional, perhaps using the therapist as a model or catalyst for these types of interactions.

Myth. Yalom gives us the idea of interpretation or theoretical construct as a sort of myth system whose importance lies in its helpfulness rather than in its truth. Schneider does not write extensively on this subject but does place importance on the subjective experience of the person in the present over a search for an ultimate truth. May suggests that myths are an appeal to a lost value-system, something held culturally in service to the individual. Frankl does not seem to contribute specifically and meaningfully on this topic. He does give us something of his personal mythology, however, in the form of his value system. In addition, the idea of post-hoc meaning can be seen as a form of adding mythology to the work, telling a story about the why of events in the past that have no actual value as truth. The value of such stories lies in its helpfulness, much like the interpretations offered by Yalom. Myth emerges again in this form in the work of Bowen, whose complex theories of Family Systems aid the therapist by providing a constructive context by which to classify and understand the data being received from a family. Satir does not seem to deal directly with this topic. Whitaker addresses myths in the relativistic fashion previously suggested. They are not helpful as static or accurate constructs, but are helpful when amenable to change (flexibility). The family's mythology impacts its rules and roles which must be fluid in order for the family to be functional; thus inflexible myths suggest inflexible rules and roles. Minuchin takes a similar stance, but is more explicit about applying a narrative intervention to the problem. That is, one helps the family tell a new and more functional story about itself, freeing up rigid rules and roles to adapt to a new context. Laing and Perls do not seem to bear directly on this issue.

Thus we have mythology as a powerful force at two levels: helping the therapist understand and classify their experiences with and of the family, and helping the family do the same for itself. Intervention at the level of making truth more relative seems to be common.

Experiental focus. Each theorist suggests that it is the lived experience of therapy (or encounter) that in some way helps the individual or family towards change. Yalom notes the healing relationship as central and the ability of the patient to try out new ways of being. Schneider implies that the ability of the therapy-goer to experience their self, their concerns and their defenses in therapy is central to their change. Frankl suggests that meaning and engagement are much the same thing. May points to courage and encounter as central to being; the implication is that a life without encounter cannot be teaching. Bowen uses his self in the role of coach, teaching by experience. Satir helps people have congruent experiences of one another and worries little about insight. Whitaker practices Symbolic Experiential therapy, and notes extensively the power of learning by doing. Minuchin also adjusts subsystems by joining them rather than by explaining them while taking a softer line on the inclusion of explicit insight (that is, being more inclined to suggest insight is necessary and pure experience is necessary, but insufficient). Laing implies that the experience of the psychotic person is all that is necessary – or indeed possible – to help with their healing. Interexperience is his main contribution in this field. Perls implies that authenticity minus engagement is meaningless; by engaging in honest encounter, one becomes more authentic.

Here we encounter the idea of simply doing in therapy. The family has already chosen to behave differently in some fashion by coming to therapy, and the therapist can be somewhat liberal about helping them to engage in ways they have not tried before. Whitaker is rather forceful in that pursuit and Minuchin implies intervention quite strongly, but Schneider suggests a more respectful, gentler movement of invitation by presence. The addition of the therapist to the system is by definition destabilizing. Perhaps no further intervention is really necessary or sufficient. This represents a divergence between Existential and Systemic thinking: while all parties concur on experience as a teacher, the degree to which one leads or facilitates varies among theorists. This will be resolved to a greater degree in the next chapter by the expedient of a value judgment from the author.

Use of self in therapy. Yalom is clear on the idea that disclosure begets disclosure, and that this disclosure must be limited to what is useful to the person rather than the therapist. He also implies that his practice of authenticity encourages the patient to try to attain the same. Schneider invites presence with presence. May implies the useful self through the amount of contemplation he has done for his writing and his art, and the amount of contemplation through which he lovingly guides his readers. Satir invites congruence with congruence and stresses the importance of being a certain type of person – a helpful, loving type. Whitaker notes the importance of being differentiated and healthy prior to embarking on a course of becoming a change agent in systemic work. Whitaker implies the same.

It is reasonably clear, although not universal, that both schools of thought require a certain amount of personal work. One must first be a certain kind of person– contemplative, interpersonally generous, differentiated, present –prior to embarking on the attempt to be helpful to others.

Reverence vs. irreverence. There is a noticeable disagreement among theorists regarding the notions of reverence and irreverence. Bowen, Minuchin, Whitaker and Frankl are notably irreverent – willing to supply direction, interpretation and commentary. Yalom straddles the line, providing these things but also explicit acceptance of the person. Schneider and Satir advocate an awe-filled appreciation of each individual that is explicitly reverent. This discontinuity crosses the bounds between Existential and Systemic thought and is not easily resolved. It is a point of disconfluence and likely contains meaning.

The difference appears to be a disagreement about the location of agency. For those advocating reverence, agency lives within each person. For those advocating directiveness (and thus irreverence), the therapist is the primary change agent. In this case, the system is being treated as though it were an entity, not necessarily conscious or willful. Each individual might retain their agency but the system is guided by the agency of the therapist.

The disagreement can probably be resolved, then, by taking a stance on agency. This dissertation will suggest that the system will evolve through the agency of its constituent parts (i.e., family members) as they learn reverence for one another and irreverence for problems, rules and roles. These latter phenomena will be seen as ways of denying or repressing what is real; people are not roles or rules but must take some active, responsible, agency-filled stance towards them.

Integration. Schneider endorses an integrative perspective; other authors do not explicitly discuss the idea. Yalom mentions Psychodynamic, Existential, Interpersonal and Group psychotherapy perspectives but in the sense of Eclectic rather than integrative practice. Frankl endorses his own methodology (Logotherapy) and only that methodology. May (as reviewed) does not spend much time on methodology at all but endorsed the Existential perspective. Bowen also stayed with his own work. Satir, Whitaker and Minuchin used various ideas from one another's and Bowen's work but contributed their own distinct ideas to their own distinct approaches. In the reading, this seems more integrative than eclectic inasmuch as the ideas contributed to one whole theory rather than mere add-on techniques to be used as convenient. Laing (as reviewed) did not discuss much methodology, and Perls stayed within the bounds of his own invention (Gestalt therapy).

Thus we have a mixture of ideas on Integration. Those with their own systems of therapy tend to avoid integrating other ideas. Family Systems therapy seems a natural integration. EI therapy is based on providing the basis for a strong integrated approach.

In the end, this idea will prove of limited applicability to ExiST, other than providing the impetus for the project.

Awe. *Existential Integrative Psychotherapy* (2008) is based on Awe and all its dimensions. Other authors relate to aspects of this phenomenon but Awe as put forward by Schneider is unique to *Existential Integrative Psychotherapy*. As such it is not included in totality in the last section. When salient, aspects of Awe are included to the extent possible, and the idea is integrated into thinking about power and its use.

Liberation. Existentialism as a psychology of liberation is an idea carried forward by Schneider and May and also implied by Frankl and Yalom. Freedom and responsibility are central ideas overlapping almost entirely with liberation. The main difference is the idea of encountering boundary territory when freedom and responsibility can be confronted directly versus experiential liberation as both goal and methodology. That is, the Ultimate Concerns are mostly encountered and a stance taken towards them, while experiential liberation is mostly lived through experience in therapy.

This idea may be related to the differentiation suggested by Bowen and the insight recommended by Minuchin. Seeing the way one behaves with a here-and-now orientation and being invited to being present to one's behavior may relate these ideas meaningfully together.

Paradox. This idea is unique to Schneider. It will not form the basis of a strong conclusion in the last section but will inform the discussion, especially in the use of power.

Presence. Presence relates to various other ideas, especially the use of self in therapy. It is endorsed specifically by Schneider and implied by Yalom and May. It is implied again by Satir, especially in the care taken with congruence and intentionality. Bowen implies it again with the idea of emotional cutoff as defense and his presence as a coach. Whitaker and Minuchin both use their feelings to inform their actions and both attend carefully to these feelings.

Presence will be a key idea, particularly Yalom's suggestion from group psychotherapy that the purpose of the therapist is not so much to relate directly to each individual but to assist the individuals in relating to one another in a way that is present. How to invite presence with presence as Schneider suggests in a family therapy format will be of some concern.

Expansion vs. contraction. To move into or withdraw from the challenges of living, to overpower or submit to one's environment, is a central conflict related to the Ultimate Concerns and also to authenticity, presence, and defenses like emotional cutoff and triangulation. While not common to other authors, this concept is foundational and informs some of the philosophical discussion in the next section as a unique and clarifying solution to a complex view of limitation and agency.

Happiness. Only Frankl explicitly mentions happiness (as reviewed) and denies it as a goal of therapy. However, his treatment of the idea reverberates with Schneider's concept of paradox, with May's idea of the Daimonic, with Whitaker's idea of craziness and Laing's concept of sane madness. Reaching for happiness is like reaching for sanity when craziness is called for. Neither is effective or warranted. To attain sanity, one must first embrace the basic sanity of insanity; to become happy, one must first live out one's unhappiness in pursuit of what is meaningful and fulfilling in life, even if that is purposeful suffering. May tells the same story with Anxiety and Angst: these are necessary madnesses that make us more human, inform our decisions, and move us towards willful and intentional behavior.

The Centrality of Being. Only May (as reviewed) discusses this philosophic issue. Thus it is not included in the following chapter as a specific part of ExiST although it does inform some of the discussion, particularly about power, will and intentionality.

By addressing the centrality of being, May seeks to make clear that it is the existential dimensions of a problem – that we are – that make the problem and all the dynamics around it possible. There are inescapable difficulties associated with being, including anxiety and suffering, which are in themselves sufficient to warrant attention. A great deal of circumlocution around these problems is, for May, unneeded and unhelpful; for example, transference is impossible and ridiculous to contemplate in the absence of human beings complete with histories and all the intellectual trappings associated with being human. That one is in this moment is all that is needed.

Family Projection Process. This and other defenses described by Bowen appear in other Systemic writings. Satir's proposed conflict between shame and self esteem and her triangles reflect Bowen's work. Minuchin's Structural theories attempt to describe these sorts of familial coping mechanisms. Whitaker's inspired interventions (directiveness) embrace the idea that these coping mechanisms are there, but do not try to analyze or identify them. Rather, Whitaker aims at change and assumes change is better than stasis. He also points out the intergenerational process and the family life cycle, which tries to perpetuate old behavior in new families.

The Existential writers do not attend to these sorts of defenses and phenomena. Yalom posits something related (merging and ultimate rescuer defenses, for example) and Schneider acknowledges the presence and necessity of defenses without being very specific about what a person's defenses might be. He assumes they will be too diverse to discuss in much detail and also implies that one's stance towards defenses (vivification) is more important than a detailed list of techniques for each defense.

In common is the use of presence, encounter and engagement and the growth into authenticity and congruence to make these defenses not necessary any longer. These will all be discussed in greater detail in the last section.

Societal Emotional Process. This refers to the presence of familial or Systemic processes outside the family. Other than implying the generalizability of ExiST outside of Family Systems work, perhaps the subject of future research, this idea is of little utility and does not appear in the next section.

Chaos vs. Homeostasis. The idea of a system defending against change by trying to force an individual to revert to old behavior is unique to Satir. The implication that a system has a life of its own presents an argument and a dilemma: whether to treat a system as a unique entity or to treat each individual as an individual.

In this debate, Minuchin votes for working with subsystems (relationships) rather than with individuals. Whitaker (as reviewed) and Bowen are silent on the issue. Yalom suggests there is a group process but that the level of intervention is with individuals via techniques such as bridging.

For the purposes of this theory, the author takes the position that the idea of a family system that can be interacted with as a separate entity is a reification. It may exist as an abstraction and it may be useful to consider in that regard (see myth, above) but does not exist in a literal sense to be intervened with or measured.

As such the level of interaction for the therapist will be rather concretely the individuals with whom they are present. One reason for this decision is philosophical – the need to reduce the reifications unique to individual brands of psychotherapy (see purpose of study and definition of problem, above). Another reason is more pragmatic: one of the most powerful interventions mentioned and common between writers is presence (or the use of self). Teaching individuals to be present to one another requires intervention at the level of individuals. The system, inasmuch as it is presumed to exist, will naturally have to accommodate to these more presence filled engagements and relationships (see Minuchin, above, and his ideas regarding intervention with subsystems). However, one cannot be present to an abstraction or invite a reification to presence through presence (at least not with any rational expectation of reciprocation).

Spirituality. Like Awe, spirituality is an ideographic idea unique to Satir. As such, it may inform some of the philosophic content in the following chapter but will not appear as its own heading.

Rules. Satir, Whitaker and Minuchin assume the existence of Rules, or implicit, rigid forms of relationship between people in a family. The rules are functional to the extent that they are flexible and relate to reality rather than to mythology.

This idea does not really have a counterpart in Existential thought or theory. However, it can be subsumed into encounter and presence; these concepts both require encountering the person and the situation in which one finds oneself rather than the ideas or judgments one has in one's imagination. In this sense, we are also discussing the sub-set of Awe in which one lives without asking, simply encountering naively whatever there is to be encountered.

Moreover, Yalom suggests the presence of transference: that old patterns of behavior and old relationships will be played out in therapy with new people, and it is the recognition of these patterns and their impacts that provides for conscious reengagement.

To the extent possible, then, it seems the Existential Systemic Therapist should help family members meet at the relative boundaries of their environments.

Pathology. Each author either takes the stance that pathology is irrelevant or takes no stance on it at all. Therefore the integrated position will assume an absence of diagnosis in this sense and presume the position of presence-ful encounter described above.

Co-therapy. This concept is unique to Whitaker. Furthermore it does not appear to add to an understanding of Systemic Theory. As such it does not appear in the following chapter.

Conclusion

There is a wealth of overlap between the ideas of the various authors reviewed here, even taking into account the unusually concise method of review employed. Very often it has been found that the differences in terminology are semantic ones: that the same thing is alluded to using differing words. Some differences have also been noted and resolved with varying degrees of success and satisfaction. While the implications of a concept to a family can vary from the implications for an individual, still there appears to be substantial basis for drawing some more solid conclusions as to the factors that might be brought to bear in ExiST.

Conclusions

The problem defined above is that Existential Psychotherapists are likely to encounter families in their work but have no or limited theoretical basis for working with this specific population. A larger and more overarching problem is the increasing diversity of theoretical approaches leading, perhaps, further away from the core principles that make therapy work.

The goal of this dissertation is to integrate Existential and Systemic thought and theory into one unified whole such that an Existential practitioner has some theoretical basis from which to practice with families. More covertly, a goal has been to demonstrate that a rational integration is possible, and to discover some basic elements of therapy in common between diverse approaches.

Thus this section will introduce the major components of ExiST. These components are authenticity, presence (encounter, relatedness, healing relationship, experiential focus, process orientation, joining the system), existential concerns, history, intentionality, and meaningfulness or engagement.

ExiST: Integrated Findings

Authenticity. Human as Vault. Imagine a powerful light surrounded by concentric rings, each ring with a narrow vertical slot. The inner ring might be one's ideals, one's most closely held truths and needs. The next ring out might be one's beliefs, and the next, one's stated beliefs and affiliations. Another ring in the outward progression might be our relational needs – for acceptance and trust and nurturance as well as for material support. The final rings are our intentions and communications: what we do, and what we say both covertly and overtly.

The light concealed within all of these rings is not really just a hot filament. It is our true self, the core of our being, and it is this core that can be of service to others. It is this core that can act upon the world positively. But most of the time it is invisible, hidden behind these concentric steel rings.

When the gaps in the rings are misaligned, a limited amount of the self is allowed into the environment (or our relationships). As the gaps come into closer and closer alignment, we begin to shine into the world with ever-increasing intensity – and this is felt by the people around us as presence.

Thus when our core beliefs and our communications and everything in between are aligned, when we are congruent, we are inordinately powerful.

The levels closer to our core are no better or worse than those further off; no hierarchy is implied in this metaphor. To approach authenticity, then, it is not always necessary to bring our action into accordance with our values. Sometimes the reverse is true: that our values need to approach our actions.

In the matter of moral learning, for example, Kohlberg [cite] posits that a person who acts out of fear of retribution or promise of reward has not attained as high a level of moral development as a person who has internalized the standards of behavior underlying their actions. Thus to not steal to avoid punishment is inauthentic if one believes stealing is right. Not stealing and coming to believe stealing is wrong would be just as authentic as establishing a career as a thief.

Authenticity as a systemic issue. Whether or not people deal directly and openly with one another is of great concern to the family system. Indirection and mystification are the enemies of healthy systems. Bowen points to triangulation and cutoff; Satir points to shame vs. self-esteem; and Minuchin identifies pathology itself as the consequence of inauthentic systems. Laing goes so far as to blame psychosis on covert forces in family systems.

By sacrificing harmony to honesty, Perls reminds us that we have to balance one with the other. In the long term, harmony bought with dishonesty is the sort of madness described above. The long-term harmony bought with authentic engagement and courage about the cost of that engagement is a stable harmony that does not incur the cost of disproportionate coping.

Authenticity in systems. Frank Herbert's (1981) *Dune* series instructs us through interwoven themes of ecology and politics to observe the flow of energy within a system; energy is always used in a way that betrays the ultimate purpose of the system. Thus authenticity can be observed at corporate levels (when their mission, vision and values match their expenditure of money); governments (when their campaign promises are kept or broken); societies (when their myths are played out in broad economic and political trends).

In families, the myths the system tells itself indicate the core values the system espouses, but its collective actions betray its core interests. Whitaker presumed this interest to be the continuation of respective families of origin; the families would be continued in the new family's way of getting things done. Satir, Bowen and Minuchin focus on the individual interests of each family member. But perhaps there are values held by the system independent of its members that may or may not relate to the individual interests of each person.

In any case, as with individual authenticity, the work is to invite the system as well as its members to greater authenticity through the act of being authentic and being present (see below). Whether the system shifts its stated values to match its actual values or its actual values to match those stated is not a matter of consequence as neither level is better than the other.

The only responsible use of power. The more powerful one is, the more capacity one has to alter the environment (and the people in it). The Taoist idea of wuwei –or, *take no action*–speaks to the dilemma of what to do with great power: to become more and more studiedly inactive. Satir notes extensively in her work that one person has no right to power over another person – even parents over children. The only responsible use of power is to teach others to come into their own power.

Schneider invites us to invite others to presence by being present to them. Laing asks us to listen to madness: the cure for psychosis is not to attempt to instill rationality but to presume it is already present and attend to it. Bowen shows us that people slavishly devoted to the emotions of others cannot escape their own associated anxiety.

Thus the authentic person is not only very intense, but also studiedly passive. Schneider instructs us to become awe-filled, to sit in reverence of the being of the other rather than to assume things about their being. Diagnosis is the application of expectations; sickness is this and thus, health is that ,and we must hurry the patient along the path towards health. This is the opposite of take no action. May gives us the deep connection between love and will; to love another is to love their intentions, their will, and saddling them with our will is counterthetical to our caring.

Van Kaam (1966) writes extensively about the ethics of influence, about helping people decide upon a change and making the change rather than pushing them towards our own ideals. Even Whitaker, who is overt and forceful in being the change agent, does not have a goal in mind for his patients except that their current state is dysfunctional, they have opted for change by visiting him, and change is represented by doing something differently. Minuchin takes a similar position, joining with the system in order to disrupt or unbalance it without a specific goal in mind in doing so except to affect change. All of these ideas relate back to Rogers's Client Centered Therapy and the core belief that the client is best served by our faith in their own basic health and competence. The major addition is the depth of ethics attached to the commitment to not use power over others but to help them come into their own power through information and will.

The extra information provided both in Systems and Existential theory is the client's impact on the therapist or other clients. The interexperience alluded to by Laing is a guidepost to intentionality. Given May's courage to encounter the suffering of others, this suffering becomes the will to behave in an authentic fashion (whatever that is).

Frankl and Whitaker are most willing of those reviewed to exert pressure on an individual or system to conform to some expectation – Frankl, to adopt a post-hoc meaning, and Whitaker to change in some (any) fashion. Otherwise, consensus seems to be on being both powerful and studiedly passive. Thus the only responsible use of power is to give it away and teach its responsible use by example.

This is ultimately a diversity issue. When the therapist begins to judge how a family should be and pushes the family along a path towards that ideal, this value judgment cannot take into account all of the variables. The Systemic therapist is likely to see people of varying nationalities and ethnic extractions, differing religious and socio-economic positions, differing ages and sexual orientations, varying lifestyles and values, geographic, political and philosophical differences, and so on.

One method used in the past to deal with diversity has been to try to catalogue and describe every sort of difference there is and work out a way to deal with it. An Existential approach to diversity is to take the opposite position: that people ought not be catalogued and typed, but experienced. In a Systemic setting, this means encountering families with very limited judgment, only inquiring and commenting on process as far as possible. Whether a son should accept an arranged marriage is not the purview of the therapist to decide; how the family discusses the subject is similarly off limits. However, the therapist can help the family understand the problem and how they encounter it so that they can make their own informed decision on how to proceed.

There are clear limits to acceptance of diversity. These limits are visible when culture and law interact. While it may be culturally acceptable for men to hit women in some countries, in the United States, this is illegal and needs to be changed. Child abuse, child pornography, terrorism, and drunk driving are all serious threats as well as serious crimes, and each has cultural implications. For example, female circumcision for religious reasons has been an issue of serious import in medical ethics in the past 10 years (e.g., Ross, 2008) as has the denial of medical care to minors on the basis of scriptural teachings. On these sorts of issues, the therapist must be more active (according to local legal and ethical standards). Of note is a recent revision to the APA code of ethics that states no psychologist may endorse or tolerate human rights abuses, potentially adding further restraint to the sorts of diversity issues that cannot be tolerated. (APA, 2010).

Presence. Many ideas and implications have been encountered regarding presence. For our purposes, we will assume presence takes place on at least three levels: physical, as in occupying the same space and time; openness, as is being receptive to whatever is present; and vulnerable, as in being willing to risk hurt (or temporary disharmony) in the service of authenticity – in other words, being unwilling to accept internal disharmony to meet the needs of the system.

To further complicate matters, presence is both an offering and a tool; it is something the therapist invites the client or family to as well as the means of invitation.

That a whole family be present physically is the subject of some disagreement. Whitaker suggests yes, as many as possible; others suggest that even a sole family member carries the whole system within their self (in the form of Ghosts). As consensus on this issue is unlikely, we will focus primarily on the more esoteric meanings of presence.

Openness. For our purposes, openness means receptivity. One of Schneider's definitions of awe is accepting the world without preconception; we care about what we see and experience without having expectations about the phenomena.

To be open to a family means to start from a position of naivety. Diagnosis, prognosis, and expectations for outcome can be tabled for the time being in the interest of merely experiencing the system as it is. Whatever the individuals want to tell us, one is open to hearing. However the system behaves, one is open to observing and experiencing. One suspends judgment but does attend to one's own feelings; these interexperiential data are important. One merely does not ascribe judgments to the feelings: anger is not bad or good; mirth is neither desirable nor lamentable. These feelings merely exist and inform one.

Vulnerability. Once one is full of interexperiential data, one might choose to share that data if the moment is right. Unlike individual therapy, the goal of sharing feelings is less to build an alliance between the system and the therapist than between members of the system; thus the sorts of disclosure that are helpful are more likely (but not necessarily, especially early in the process) about one's observations of others within the system. Someone appears bored or listless, angry or impatient; someone's voice quavered as they approached a particular topic. Inquiries about how each person feels about each other person begin to move the process forward. One could view the expression of affect as the revelation of a secret; horizontal disclosure about the secret can be a tool to deepen contact between members of the system.

Metanarrative. There is a metanarrative implied by these presences: that openness and vulnerability are good, that authenticity is good. Indeed presence and authenticity are core values of the Existential approach and impossible to conceal.

Thus care must be taken in the application of presence and authenticity that it is not a technique, but a way of being. Minuchin's idea of spontaneity applies here. One avoids manipulation and forcefulness by being powerful and taking studied inaction. Thus this way of being is merely available, on display, another potential or option in a universe filled with potentials and options.

Thus before engaging in presenceful encounters in the therapy room, one must become a presenceful person outside of it. A contemplative lifestyle, be it through spiritual engagements, a deep concern with nature, connectedness to literature or philosophy, or one's own therapy, is truly necessary prior to these sorts of encounters.

Presence to the process. A strong process-orientation is common to most of the theory reviewed thus far. Using observations about what is happening as well as to whom it is happening may be useful. This fosters insight as well as fostering insight about how to foster insight (that is, each intervention comprises a sort of metanarrative, in which the mode of the intervention points to the values of the therapist).

Most of the theorists reviewed agree that the problem is not the problem; rather, how the individuals or systems engage the problem is the problem. Thus, the content of any given conversation or encounter is unlikely to be of clinical or therapeutic interest. Rather, how the system talks about what it talks about, how it does what it does, or even that it does so is likely to be more productive territory.

It is necessary to not only experience and comment upon the system but to join the system. Just as the therapist becomes an ally to the patient, the Systemic therapist must become an ally to the family, a companion along their road for a time. The ideal therapist has become quite individuated and is careful of the tides within the system and also takes a dual perspective: from within and without, keeping both perspectives in mind at the same time (as in Schneider asking us to be present both to the person in the room and to the immensity of being all around us).

Where Minuchin suggests only positive feedback from within the system, the Existential approach advocates care for the Daimonic. As Elkins (2010) states, one must be willing to paint with the black sand as well as with all the cheerful colors, because the human condition is one in which we hurt others and are hurt by them. Thus the Existential Systemic approach to being an ally includes examining all the hurts and misdeeds as well as the way the system is wonderful.

This is a major point of departure between Existentialism and Systemic thinking. Satir thought every person was a wonderful being; her deep belief of this wonderfulness is cited as a core factor in her success as a therapist. The Existentialist, however, is more likely to suspend judgment concerning wonderfulness or hatefulness and accept that the person is wondrous (that is, sufficient provocation to awe and naivety).

The point of confluence might be a general reluctance to reject people for their faults. Even for the Existentialist, the pointing out of the black sand is done in a careful fashion, without blaming or demands for restitution. Like Minuchin's rules, this is done lovingly and in the service of insight for, as May contends, one is responsible only inasmuch as one knows the facts: to see the suffering of another being makes one responsible to one's values in a way one was not before observing the suffering.

Healing. It has been contended many times in the course of this research that it is the power of encounter and relatedness that heals in and of itself. Yalom has gone so far as to state that everything else we do in therapy just gives us something to do while the relationship is working. In the case of Systemic work, one might make the same contention.

That the family is related is a given, and why is not strictly relevant (or is at least tautological). How they relate to one another, however, is the area of concern as clearly illustrated in the second section. Even the Existentialists contend that a well-related person is a healthier person with a more meaningful life; one might assume a family of healthier people would constitute a healthier family.

Thus the major healing factor in Systemic work is less the individual family members' relationships with the therapist than their relationships with one another. One's goal might be to help the family members be able to do for one another what the therapist does for an individual. As suggested by combining Schneider and Yalom, above, the only intervention necessary to make this happen is to invite the members of the family to one another's presence through bridging.

Existential Concerns. Part of life is engagement in the world as it is. Psychopathology can be related to attempts to evade the more difficult truths of existence, such as death and responsibility. In family systems, those truths might (or might not) be more immediate concerns; in triangulation, it is our conflict with a person who can influence one's feelings in some way that one avoids. Isolation is not a given in this case but its opposite, as one seeks to isolate one's feelings from the perceived source of harm, to become less vulnerable.

Thus the givens of existence for family systems, the unavoidable ultimate concerns, might be different than those posited by Yalom (above). They probably include the family life cycle and all the events contained therein: death, literal and figurative, looms large. Another family given might include an aspect of relatedness and Heidigger's thrownness: one cannot choose one's family of origin. We are born into a particular family situation without our consent. The system, too, might experience a sort of thrownness as it comes to consciousness in a particular society, geography, historical context and political situation. Next is likely a form of limited will; as one becomes conscious of the system of which one is a part, one also becomes more or less aware of one's choicefulness of action within the context of the system. The system itself may have its own collective will (see chaos, above, for example) against which an individual might battle.

History. A here-and-now, process orientation does not rule out the collection of history. However, the way history is understood is another matter. There are essentially two ways of understanding history: either understanding the present in terms of the past, or understanding the past in terms of the present. In the former case, present behavior and experience is understood as created (determined) by past events. It can therefore be used to excuse or pigeonhole behavior. It cannot be changed or adapted, and leads away from a process-oriented, here-and-now, experiential focus.

Memory is in any case a fabrication (e.g., Perls, 1981) and not very trustworthy. Any family history ought to be construed as a sort of myth and used as such. When one attempts to understand the past in terms of the present, one focuses on the present aspects of the past. How the system feels about it, uses it and understands it all become grist for the here-and-now mill. The past is no longer something that has determined the present, but something in the present which can be responded to. While the past cannot be changed, the way the family understands, feels about and uses the past can be changed in the present.

Thus the idea of horizontal disclosure returns to the field. When examining the past, the job of the therapist is not to simply hear stories about history, but to help the family disclose present events around that story-telling.

Intentionality. Everyone has resistances and self-protections. The reason is that they are needed; people cannot be aware every moment of the looming specter of death (limitation) or bear the continual pressure of coping for one's family system.

A goal in Existential Psychotherapy is to help people become more aware of their resistances and self-protections in order that they can choose whether and how to enact these protections. An assumption tied to this vivification is that people, when actively choosing their defenses, will tend to choose defensive behavior that is more functional and less damaging than if they defend without consciousness.

In Systemic work, very much of an individual's interaction in a family is taken to be defensive (or coping) behavior: not only triangulation but its consequences; not only the family projection process, but the pathology of the child onto whom the process has been projected; not only the incongruent metacommunication but the coping style that follows.

A good piece of ExiST, then, must focus on the intentionality of behavior. Getting to intentionality has several stages: first, developing awareness (of situation, of feelings, and of desires); second, making a decision that is functional for the individual; third, enacting one's decision.

Awareness. Awareness can be fostered through many of the methods already reviewed. Process comments focus the person on awareness of the context, the ebb and flow of energy within the family system. Bridging helps build empathy between members of the system, such that a family member can become aware of how others feel and, through sharing one's own feelings, aware of those feelings more deeply and more in the moment. Once these awarenesses are fostered (context and feelings) what is left is desires.

Desires or needs or wishes are the beginnings of will and are begun by will. At the individual level, one's wishes most likely contain not only self-oriented content (the need for honesty or self-protection, for actualization or dependency) but also system-oriented material (the need for harmony or altruism). Ultimately, however, the system-level need can be understood at the individual level; the need for harmony can be understood as the need to avoid anxiety or shame or to procure positive feedback, for example.

Such needs can be elucidated through the bridging process. Once the feelings are understood (and a safe space has been created for sharing such personal data, a process that may take substantial time), desires can be discussed by the same means. Getting family members to inquire about one another's needs can be a helpful exercise inasmuch as it gets those needs out into the open but also by the metanarrative of learning to value the needs of others in a non-enmeshed context.

Making a decision. Decisions constitute boundary territory (Yalom, 2003/2009). This means that the act of making a decision brings one into direct contact with the ultimate concerns: saying yes to one thing, for example, is equivalent to saying no to all other things. This death of potential as a figurative death is a powerful symbol for actual death. Freedom and responsibility are obviously in play – a decision must be made freely or it does not constitute a decision, and once made, its maker is responsible for the outcome. Inasmuch as meaningfulness can be said to be a derivation of engagement and decision is engagement with living, meaningfulness is also encountered here. Finally, in the context of ExiST, every decision will have relational import, bringing us around to isolation.

This manuscript posits a relationship between isolation, responsibility and differentiation. The undifferentiated person is ultimately unfree. As the choice to become more differentiated is presented, this differentiation carries overtones of reduced connectedness, of reduced enmeshment. One will begin to have only one's own thoughts and feelings to respond to. One will become increasingly alone. The thought that one will also become increasingly oneself, that the space within that is currently occupied with coping with the system's various anxieties will become occupied with one's own capacities and potentialities, may not be available. The decision, then, is significant boundary territory in a way that may be less accessible in individual or group Existential practice.

The therapist must be cognizant of the import of a decision and be ready to nurture and foster the person through the process. If the Existential process is mostly about being aware of themes that are already present in psychotherapy then, rather than calling the individual's attention to the Existential aspect of the decision, the therapist need merely listen for it, attune to it, and stand ready to be of help (by helping the family be of help).

The decision an individual makes may be to act against individuation or to continue a pathology. The Existential Systemic therapist is faced with the awareness that the individual must choose not only for themselves, but also for the system of which they are a part. The Systemic authors noted above would tend to value differentiation (by whatever name) over continued enmeshment. The Existential Systemic therapist might be more careful to value the process of deciding over the actual decision made, particularly in the face of adequate information and capacity to consent.

Authenticity is not synonymous with differentiation. Often, there are competing needs and desires at every level of being; the need to maintain harmony against the need for honesty, for example. This conflict might be resolved in either direction with equal authenticity, depending on the depth of value on either side of the equation. Hypothetically, someone lying to their family about their sexual orientation might not suffer very much if they really believed that the lie was in service of the greater good.

Enacting a decision. Next, the individual must enact their decision in some fashion. In family systems language, to enact means to put into play in the therapy session. Ideally, the therapy room by now has become a safe place to try out different behavior and different ways of being. If it is not safe to do so, therapy is unlikely to proceed beneficially as attempts to create change will be met with attempts to preserve homeostasis in dysfunctional fashions (such as abuse or recrimination).

When a new behavior is enacted, there will likely be a form of negative chaos. In chaos, a conditioned behavior no longer meets with the expected maintaining consequence; people try to get the maintaining consequence by repeating the behavior and increasing intensity. The posited negative chaos is a reverse situation: one is trying out a new behavior for which one has no data – one does not know what consequence to expect, and others present do not know how to respond to it.

This is a key time for positive feedback. When the person engages in the new action, they can find out from the family whether or not it was functional. The therapist can use bridging to help the individual get more data and also to begin horizontal disclosure – that is, to find out what made it possible to engage in the new behavior, and what responses they liked from their family.

When possible, the therapist might try to ensure that positive praise comes from the family rather than from the therapist in order to slow down the process of fostering dependency. Here we have described a sort of experiential liberation: the freedom to choose how one participates in the family process with full information about the consequences of that choice. Care must be taken to defend and consolidate that liberation as it happens, to foster and protect it, even–especially-against the therapist.

Thus by enacting a decision – trying on a new way of being in the therapy room – the person can move on to the next decision-making process: whether or not to continue the new way of being outside the therapy room.

Meaningfulness: ExiST as a Psychology of Engagement

The idea of myths has been put forward on various levels. Minuchin is clearest in writing on myth inasmuch as the myth must serve the family rather than the family serving the myth. The myth must be flexible and useful. If it is present but blocking change, it is like a read-only memory on a computer; one cannot interact with it. If it is flexible, then one can encounter or engage with the myth.

This engagement brings the family closer to authenticity (much the same as interacting with the idea of the ideal self brings the self closer; either the ideal or the behavior can change). Meaning can be construed as living a life that is meaningful: living in accordance with one's values. Thus living in accordance with the family myths would be meaningful for the family, and myth flexibility allows this to happen functionally.

Emotional cutoff, triangulation and incongruence are all forms of detachment from reality. An individual avoids a stressor but the stressor remains; an individual avoids one's anxiety, but the anxiety remains and is communicated through another relationship; one avoids one's angst and does not speak of it openly but communicates it via metacommunications. Becoming open and engaged means not only engaging with one's family, with the shared sources of anxiety, but also with one's self. The individual must become aware of the stressors in the system and engage with them actively, and also become aware of and engaged with the stressors within the individual.

Systemic authenticity is reached, then, by individual authenticity, and this is reached by a process of engagement. Meaning can further be construed as experiences of the self and other, as encounters that are authentic and moving. Here again, meaningfulness is attained through engagement.

Presence to the other means, by and large, encounter with the actual person inasmuch as is possible in the presence of our human limitations. This means laying aside our preconceptions and expectations and allowing the other to impact us in some fashion, to provoke and promote responses and change. Engagement is in the mutual sharing of interexperience. Another construal of meaning is this type of encounter, this relatedness.

At each step, meaningfulness is revealed not so much as a goal to be grasped and added into the system as a consequence of various levels of engagement: with myth (narrative meaning), with intentionality, with the other, with the self.

The Process Unified

ExiST as distilled from these readings is a series of stances or attitudes rather than a series of procedures to follow or things to do. It is assumed that the practitioner of ExiST is trained and properly certified or supervised to perform family therapy and thus already knows what to do; it would be hoped that the practitioner will find these stances informative.

The first stance is a modified form of the Humanistic belief in the essential fitness of the family to find their own solutions. Existentially speaking, this belief is modified to include the possibility that the family – or the individuals therein – are capable of not only good choices but of evil ones.

The next stance is the belief that each person is free: to choose either good or evil, to utilize or abnegate their own freedom, to accept consequences or shift blame, to hear or disregard information. While each human has the capacity to heal theirselves some may decide not to do so. This is the essence of freedom. And with this freedom naturally comes responsibility. While it can be denied it, like freedom, is never really lost.

Next is the belief that the more power one has, the more one is responsible to stay one's hand. Exerting one's power over a system is to render that system powerless to the same degree. Having acknowledged the family's capacity, freedom and responsibility, the therapist becomes increasingly still with regard to the system, promoting responsible action through take-no-action.

The fourth stance is one of presence. The therapist invites the family to be present to one another by being present to each individual and to each member and directly fostering that presence through activities such as bridging. This presence requires encountering each individual and each relationship in a clear and unidealized manner.

Fifth is the stance of awe: of an awareness of things as they are, both beautiful and dreadful; of an encounter with the family without preconceptions or labels; of a sense of wonderment and non-attachment (or absence of expectation).

Sixth and last is the stance of being. The past and the future may be salient but are ultimately imaginary; the time when decisions are possible is now. Thus the ExiST therapist adopts a here-and-now stance. Inquiry focuses on the present moment. When the subject is a time other than the present, the inquiry regards the effect of that other time on the present moment.

Assumptions and Limitations

This dissertation has examined English-speaking practitioners and theorists, largely as a convenience to the author but also with regard to the fairly specific cultural adaptations of therapy vis-à-vis the American individual ego and family system. Existential therapy alludes to universal truths of human existence (e.g., Yalom's Givens) but how these universals play out across cultures is unknown. Indeed, how they play out even in the rich tapestry of American cultures is largely unexamined. A beginning was made by various authors in Schneider (2008), especially in the chapters on multiculturalism by Comas-Diaz (2008), Rice (2008), and Alsup (2008), but this is the barest beginning.

Thus a limitation will be that the author of this dissertation is an individual with individual experiences of his cultures and identities; an examination of the subjects discussed here from other perspectives might yield very different results. Indeed, such an examination would undoubtedly prove profitable to the field of study and thus is highly encouraged.

Another key limitation is the author's interest in both Existential and Family Systems, as stated above. In desiring a rational methodology, it may be that the author sees connections where none is really present or relevant. Indeed, the literature review from the Family Systems' side of the equation intentionally neglects those theorists with no perceived connection to the subject at hand, and has in turn not extensively examined material from the included authors that did not seem directly germane. As the author has little interest in proving that there is only one way or a best way, those authors who can be understood clearly in Existential terms have been deemed most valuable in elucidating the theory and the rest gently ignored for the time being.

This project also contains some basic assumptions. First, that Existential psychology is a useful treatment modality (one among many such modalities). Secondly, that Family Systems therapy is also useful. Thirdly, that Existential Psychotherapists might encounter families in their work. Last, that it is possible to integrate the two and that the integration will result in synthesis, as it has in other fields, such as art therapy and music therapy. Indeed, the author's bias that integration is better than segregation is sufficiently deeply ingrained that even awareness of the bias helps little in seeing another point of view.

Learning from the Process: Personal Notes

This part of the paper diverges slightly from standard APA format in order to convey the author's experiences and learnings during the process of writing this dissertation. The author will digress briefly into a first-person format for the purpose of this discussion.

I have struggled for three years with the ideas contained in these writings. I have at times embraced the Existential framework for psychotherapy and at times have tried out other sorts of methodology. Overridingly, Existentialism has always exerted a pull and supplanted other ways of doing business for me.

During the time I was writing this dissertation, I have had contact with many individuals considered important in this field and have allowed myself to be open to their collective influences. I have increasingly pursued Existentialism not just as a treatment modality or as a philosophy but also as a means to satisfy a spiritual hunger I was not even aware of until recently.

Also, this project was completed during my internship year during which I had several opportunities to actually practice family therapy and integrate these inquiries into that practice. While not a part of the research conducted for this dissertation, the experiences have been invaluable and have added substantial heft to the "why" portions of the inquiry.

Doing the reading, which was not insubstantial, I learned to guide my inquiries by trusting my feelings. Some material would bring tears to my eyes, although it was not necessarily emotional reading. Other material would make me laugh joyously out loud, while containing no punchline or absurdity. These were ultimately the materials that guided me into a deeper perspective, a wiser understanding of the processes at hand. Readings that did not prompt such affective responses I discarded along the way, really winnowing the field to what has been presented in this text.

Thus one major lesson out of conducting this research is that I ought to research meaningfully, which, in this context, meaningfully means engagedly. That which is engaging contains wisdom; that which is not engaging contains merely information.

Another key lesson is that I am capable of this level of discourse. This is the longest effort of sustained attention I have ever completed, including two unpublished novels I wrote as a teenager. I had begun to despair of ever being able to write at that level again until finally mustering the will to complete this project. It has been exceptionally daunting at times and clearly very rewarding to me.

One of the internal struggles involved has been wrestling with my own sense of myself. There is a certain arrogance involved in taking the position of 'expert.' I liken being in this role to balancing on a chair with three legs: the position is unstable and necessarily temporary. Thus the audacity of taking on a project as big as a dissertation – tantamount to wishing to become a doctor – seemed initially to be well above my humble aspirations. I thought at some level that I must be punished if I were to try to rise so far above my perceived station. Along the way, I have written a book (self-referenced jokingly elsewhere in this manuscript), completed an internship, become an international presenter and ambassador for Existentialism of modest stature, and really started to learn what it is that I am about as a Psychologist, as a Psychotherapist, and as this human being who exists independently of these roles.

At the last, though, this thing I have written is offered humbly, with humility, and with great thanks to all those who have helped in its – and in my own – development.

More concretely, I intended this work to be two dissertations in one. Firstly, it is about what it says it is about, namely the integration of two methods of psychotherapy for which I have developed an affection and an affinity. Second, more covertly, it is about the process of integration. Like good therapy, this dissertation contains a subtext that has little or nothing to do with its content. It is my hope that, however much any given reader approves or disapproves of the content, that the process will be clear and will survive much further into the future than ExiST does.

Future Research

A fruitful inquiry, according to scientific philosophy, is fecund: that is, it raises questions, spurs new research, and leads to new avenues of investigation. Thus this section considers the manner in which this dissertation may contribute directions of further inquiry.

The triggering event for this research was the desire of the author to qualitatively or quantitatively examine the impact of Existentialism on Systemic practice, and finding no theory on which to hang any questions. Thus this theoretical paper provides the opportunity to ask, is ExiST efficacious? And, how do families whose therapist uses ExiST experience their time in therapy, or how do ExiST therapists experience the families with whom they work?

The author also wonders about therapist factors. Existentialism is a philosophical movement that developed more recently into a method of therapy. What sort of person is it who is helpful to people, and how does engagement with depth philosophy contribute to the development of a depth therapist? Moreover, one might ask the same questions with regard to Systemic therapists.

From a more process-oriented perspective comes the question: what other forms of therapy can be productively integrated in this fashion? Given the breadth and depth of the problem as defined above, there remain too many competing practices leading further away from the fundamental common factors that make therapy effective. Can more such factors be discovered or corroborated by this method?

A remaining question when one considers the nature of efficacy research is, what does it mean to be effective? Given a sort of goalless stance, a take-no-action ethic that honors the needs of the family to engage their own Existential freedom, how would one go about goal-setting? Given a fundamental disbelief in (or at least disregard for) psychopathology, what illnesses could be treated in a double-blind clinical study in order to prove the worth of therapy? What are the ultimate goals of a type of therapy that largely eschews these sorts of inquiry, and what measures could account for efficacy along these sorts of axes?

Conclusion

This dissertation contributes to therapy literature by deepening the understanding of central concepts in existential and systemic theories by putting them in the context of dialogue. The same concept in a new context helps one to understand nuances of the ideas that were previously obscured.

For example, the dialogue between presence and the therapist as a tool of therapeutic change deepens our understanding of what it is to be present to people in a way that is healing; the dialogue between authenticity and congruence helps create an understanding of authenticity that accounts for myth, diversity needs, backgrounds, and family process. In doing this, a new understanding has been reached that makes these concepts more useful in more areas of specialty.

In addition, this work has shown that a well-intentioned attempt to create this sort of fusion can succeed and can find fundamental, foundational concepts to serve us in the therapeutic endeavor.

This project began with the search for some sort of general principles of psychotherapy, some version of $E=mc^2$. Very complex ideas in the second section have resolved into simpler ones in the fourth and still simpler ones in the beginning of this section. The next paragraphs continue the project of distilling ever-simpler principles from complex observations.

The Existential method is really one of becoming the sort of person who is helpful to other people, specifically to people in some sort of psychological distress. Across all of the readings on this subject, it is quite difficult to encounter procedures, directions, or techniques. Students can become frustrated pursuing the notion of an Existential Psychotherapy for this reason. The technique really seems to boil down to this notion alone: become a helpful person and then be with people.

ExiST might boil down to this identical notion: become a person who is helpful to families and then be with families.

The author has this last piece of advice for those wishing to learn to practice ExiST: read this dissertation very carefully, take fruitful notes, encounter your own questions about it, consider your emotional reactions to it and, at the last, forget it.

References

Alsup, R. (2008). Existentialism of personalism: a Native American perspective. In Schneider

    (ed.). *Existential integrative psychotherapy: Guideposts to the core of practice.* pp. 121-

    129. New York: Routledge.

American Psychiatric Association. (2000). *Diagnostic and statistical manual of mental disorders*

    (Revised 4th Ed.). Washington, DC: Author.

American Psychological Association (2010). *Code of ethics.* Retrieved 6/16/10 from

    http://www.apa.org/ethics/code/index.aspx.

Baldwin, M. (1999). *The use of self in therapy.* New York: Haworth Press.

Barth, R. (1990). *Theories guiding home-based intensive family preservation service.* In Booth,

    C., Elizabeth, T., Kinney, J., & Whittaker, J., (Eds.). *Reaching high-risk families:*

    Intensive family preservation in human services (modern applications of social

    work). New Jersey: Aldine Transaction.

Becker, E. (1966/1997). *The denial of death.* New York: The Free Press.

Bowen, M. (1978). *Family treatment in clinical practice.* New York: Jason Aronson.

Brallier, J., & Parker, R. (2002). *Who was Albert Einstein?* New York: Grosset and

    Dunlap.

Brothers, B. (1991). *Virginia Satir: foundational ideas.* New York: Haworth Press.

Bugental, J. (1981). *The search for authenticity: An existential-analytical approach to psychotherapy*. New York: Irvington Publishers.

Comas-Diaz, L. (2008). Latino psychospirituality. In Schneider (ed.). *Existential*

integrative

psychotherapy: Guideposts to the core of practice. pp. 100-110. New York:

Routledge.

Crown, S., Freeman, H., & Freeman, H. (1993). *The book of psychiatric books.* New

Jersey: Jason Aronson, Inc.

Dias, J. (2010). *Paintings in sand.* Colorado Springs: Dias Family Press.

Duhl & Duhl (1991). Integrative family therapy. In Gurman, A., & Kniskern, D., (Eds.),

Handbook of family therapy, I, pp 483-517. New York: Brunner/Mazel.

Elkins, D. (2009). *Humanistic psychology: A clinical manifesto.* Colorado: University

of the Rockies Press.

Elkins, D. (2010). An afterword that is actually a foreword. In Dias, J. (2010).

Paintings in sand. Colorado: Dias Family Press.

Frankl, V. (2006). *Man's search for meaning.* Massachusetts: Beacon Street Press.

Herbert, F. (1981). *God emperor of Dune.* New York: Putnam.

Hoffman, L. (2009). Introduction to existential psychology in a cross-cultural context: an

East-West dialogue. In Hoffman, L. & Yang, M., (Eds.) 2009. *Existential*

psychology East-West. Colorado: University of the Rockies Press.

Keith, D., & Whitaker, W. (1991). Symbolic experiential family therapy. In Gurman,

A., & Kniskern, D., (Eds.) 1991. *Handbook of family therapy, volume I.* pp 483-

517. New York: Brunner/Mazel.

Laing, R. (1960). *The divided self.* New York: Penguin.

Laing, R. (1961). *Self and others.* New York: Pantheon.

Laing, R., Esterton, A. (1964). *Sanity, madness and the family.* New York: Penguin.

Laing, R. (1967). *The politics of experience.* New York: Pantheon Books.

May, R. (1950/1996). *The meaning of anxiety.* New York: Norton.

May, R. (1994). *The courage to create.* New York: Norton.

May, R., (1969). *Love and will.* New York: Delta.

May, R. (1983). *The discovery of being.* New York: Norton.

May, R. (1989). *Freedom and destiny.* New York: Delta.

Mendelowitz, E. (2008). *Ethics and Lao Tzu:Intimations of character.* Colorado:

    University of the Rockies Press.

Minuchin, S. (1974). *Families and family therapy.* Cambridge: Harvard University

    Press.

Minuchin, S. (1984). *The family kaleidoscope.* Cambridge: Harvard University Press.

Minuchin, S., and Fishman, C. (1981). *Family therapy techniques.* Cambridge: Harvard

    University Press.

Minuchin, S. and Nichols, M.P. (1999). *Family healing: Tales of hope and renewal from*

    family therapy. New York: The Free Press.

Napier, A., Whitaker, C. (1978). *The family crucible.* New York: Harper and Row.

Perls, F. (1969/1992). *Gestalt therapy verbatim.* Maine: The Gestalt Journal Press

Perls, F. (1981). *In and out of the garbage pail.* New York: Bantam.

Pierson, J., and Schneider, K. (2009). J. Fraser Pierson and the awe of natural living. In

    Schneider, K. (2009). *Awakening to awe: Personal stories of profound*

    transformation.

New Jersey: Jason Aronson, Inc.

Rice, D. (2008). An African American perspective: The case of Darrin. In Schneider (Ed.). *Existential integrative psychotherapy: Guideposts to the core of practice* pp. 110-121. New York: Routledge.

Ross, S. (2008). *Women's human rights: The international and comparative law casebook.* Pittsburgh: University of Pennsylvania Press. p. 509.

Satir, V. (1983). *Conjoint family therapy.* California: Science and Behavior Books.

Satir, V. (1988). *The new peoplemaking.* California: Science and Behavior Books.

Satir, V., Banmen, J., Gerber, J., and Gomori, M. (1991). *The Satir model: Family therapy and beyond.* California: Science and Behavior Books.

Satir, V. (1991). *Making contact.* California: Celestial Arts.

Satir, V. M., & Bitter, J. R. (2000). The therapist and family therapy: Satir's human validation process model. In A. M. Horne (Ed.), *Family therapy and counseling (3rd Ed..)* p. 62-101. Illinois: F. E. Peacock.

Schneider, K. (2008). *Existential integrative psychotherapy.* New York: Routledge.

Schneider, K. (2004). *Rediscovery of awe: Splendor, mystery and the fluid center of life.* Utah: Paragon.

Schneider, K. (2009). *Awakening to awe: Personal stories of profound transformation.* New Jersey: Jason Aronson, Inc.

Schneider, K. (1993). *Horror and the holy: Wisdom teachings of the monster tale.* Chicago: Open Court Publishing.

Sheffield, E. (2004). Beyond abstraction: Philosophy as a practical qualitative research method. *The qualitative report, 9,* 760-769.

Van Kaam, A. (1966). *The art of existential counseling: A new perspective in psychotherapy.* Wilkes-Barre: Dimension Books.

Wampold, B. (2001). *The great psychotherapy debate.* New York: Lawrence Erlbaum.

Whitaker, C. (1981). Symbolic-experiential family therapy. In A. S. Gurman & D. P. Knistern (Eds.), *Handbook of family therapy* (p. 187-225). New York: Brunner/Mazel.

Yalom, I. (1980). *Existential psychotherapy.* New York: Basic Books.

Yalom, I. (1996). *Lying on the couch.* New York: HarperPerennial.

Yalom, I. (2005). *Theory and practice of group psychotherapy,* (5th Ed.). New York: Basic Books.

Yalom, I. (2005). *When Nietzsche wept: A novel of obsession.* New York: Perennial Classics.

Yalom, I. (2003/2009). *The gift of therapy.* New York: Harper Collins.

www.ingramcontent.com/pod-product-compliance
Lightning Source LLC
Chambersburg PA
CBHW081148280526
45787CB00008B/3252